CULTURAL HERITAGE OF MATHURA

A BIBLIOGRAPHY

CULTURAL HERITAGE OF MATHURA

A BIBLIOGRAPHY

Edited by
JAGDISH S. YADAV

MANOHAR
AMERICAN INSTITUTE OF INDIAN STUDIES
1991

ISBN 81-85425-56-6

First Published 1991

Published by Ajay Kumar Jain, Manohar Publications
2/6 Ansari Road, Darayaganj, New Delhi 110 002
for
American Institute for Indian Studies
D-31 Defence Colony, New Delhi 110 024

Lasertypeset by A.J. Software Publishing Co. Pvt. Ltd.,
305, Durga Chambers,, 1333, D.B. Gupta Road,
Karol Bagh, New Delhi 110 005

Printed at Rajkamal Electric Press,
B35/9, G.T. Karnal Road Ind. Area, Delhi 110 033

Dedicated
to
Fredrick M. Asher

CONTENTS

FOREWORD

I am pleased to introduce to scholars of Indology the scientific and extensive Bibliography of works on Mathura, otherwise known as *Cultural Heritage of Mathura: A Bibliography* compiled by Mr. Jagdish S. Yadav, my dearest friend and colleague.

The culture of Mathura remains one of the most fascinating and important areas of Indological research. Its distinctive art style is known by its name which has exercised great influence on the course of Indian art history. A study of Indian art without reference to Mathura is simply unimaginable. In view of its cultural importance AIIS organized an International seminar on Mathura in 1980 and the papers presented at the seminar have been published by the Institute under the title *Mathura: The Cultural Heritage*.

Mathura's glorious past although repeatedly narrated in the early Indian literature, remained concealed in the womb of the earth for several centuries until Col. Stacy discovered the first antiquity in 1836. Since then thousands of terracottas, coins, sculptures and architectural remains have been discovered which can be seen in the Museums of Indian art all over the world. A large number of research papers, monographs and books covering various aspects of cultural heritage of Mathura have been published. The need of a Bibliography on the subject has been, therefore, very much felt by the researchers and the present work will, I am sure, immensely fulfil that need. The material has been systematically arranged according to the Subject Index, Author Index and Keyword Index. I trust the publication of this volume will serve a great cause and will be welcomed by scholars working on any aspect of ancient Mathura in particular and Indian art and culture in general.

On my own behalf and on behalf of the AIIS, I congratulate Mr. Yadav on this excellent compilation.

5 September 1991 — P.R. Mehendiratta
New Delhi — Director

PREFACE

Mathura occupies a very distinguished place in the history and culture of India as an active centre of Brahmanism, Buddhism and Jainism for several centuries. Its distinctive art style is known by its name which has exercised great influence on the course of Indian art history. No study of Indian art or religion is, therefore, complete without a study of Mathura. The rich sites within the city of Mathura and its vicinity have yielded hundreds of terracottas, coins, sculptures and architectural remains, which can be seen in the museums of Indian art all over the world.

In view of its importance, The American Institute of Indian Studies organised an International Seminar on Mathura in 1980. The papers presented at the Seminar have now been published by the Institute under the title *Mathura: The Cultural Heritage*. There is a lot of published literature on Mathura covering all the major aspects, such as history, society, religion, archaeology, epigraphy, numismatics, art, iconography and sculpture, etc. But there is no comprehensive bibliography of this vast published material. This bibliography aims to fill this gap.

The bibliography is divided into three parts in the following sequence:

(i) Classified Subject Index

(ii) Author Index

(iii) Key-Word Index

CLASSIFIED SUBJECT INDEX: All books and articles have been classified according to the subjects mentioned in the 'Contents'. Each entry in this part has been serialised for cross reference in indexes (ii) and (iii). The names of authors in each subject-group are alphabetically arranged beginning with the surname followed by name (in full or initials). If references about Mathura figure on a large number of pages in a particular book, then the information concerning the book alone is given. In case of the articles dealing with Mathura are in the collected works (Felicitation, Commemoration, Seminar-proceedings, etc.) or journals, then fuller details including the page-numbers are given. Examples of a few entries in the classified Subject Index are presented below:

Asher, Frederick M.
The art of Eastern India, 300-800. Minneapolis,
The University of Minnesota. Press, 1980

In this entry, author's surname is given first, followed by forename, title of the book, place of publication, publisher and year of publication. Since references about Mathura figure on many pages of this publication, these pages have not been mentioned in the entry.

Huntington, John C.
Mathura evidence for the early teachings of
Mahayana. In Doris Meth Srinivasan, ed.,
Mathura: The Cultural Heritage. New Delhi,
American Institute of Indian Studies, 1989: 85-92

In this case, an articie dealing with Mathura is in a collected work. Hence the complete information about the author's name, title of the article, editor of the collected work, title of the collected work, place of publication, publisher, year of publication, and the page numbers on which this article appeared are given.

Another example:

Sharma, R.C.
New Inscriptions from Mathura.
Bulletin of Museums & Archaeology in U.P.,
No. 8, December 1971: 24-28.

Here author's name, title of the article, name of the journal in which this article was published, the issue number of the journal, year of publication and pages on which this article appeared are given.

AUTHOR INDEX: An Author Index is provided to locate an author's contributions irrespective of any subject-group. The names of the authors have been alphabetically arranged by surname followed by first name. The entries have been numbered serially in Classified Subject Index and these entry numbers are mentioned against the name of each author. For example:

Agrawala, V.S., 1-5, 139, 210-211, 302-305, 723-749, 1004-1013, 1132-1136, 1206-1210, 1258-1261.

Joshi, N.P., 150, 275, 843-853, 1050-1068, 1227-1228, 1273, 1313.

All book and articles by V.S. Agrawala and N.P. Joshi are listed at serial numbers mentioned against their names in the Classified Subject Index.

KEY-WORD INDEX: The Classified Subject Index has been supplemented by a Key-Word Index. Sometimes it is difficult to classify an article or a book, particularly when it deals with more than one subject. To help scholars to find an article or book on any subject covered in this bibliography, this part should prove very useful. Important key-words from the titles of the books and journals listed in this bibliography have been selected and listed in an alphabetical order. This is not done if the key-word and subject group are same. For example, if epigraphy is the key-word and this book or article is listed in the subject-group Epigraphy, then the key-word Epigraphy has not been selected because all the articles dealing with Epigraphy will be found in the subject-group Epigraphy. But if the Key-word is Epigraphy and this book or article is not listed in the subject-group Epigraphy, then this key-word is selected. Against each key-word, serial numbers of the Classified Subject Index are given. For example:

Kaniska, 14, 19, 39, 86, 89, 98, 131, 319, 372, 413, 444, 470, 530, 544, 580, 623, 630, 659, 759, 868, 874, 954, 981, 1023, 1189-1190.

Kankali Tila, 114, 275, 330, 348, 350, 436, 496, 506.

Mahisasuramardini, 994, 1003, 1043, 1079, 1083, 1129, 1264.

Mauryas, 17, 25, 35, 88, 129, 140, 423, 549, 572, 667, 915-916, 1265, 1301.

An attempt has been made to make the bibliography as comprehensive as possible within the framework of the above-discussed structure. It is hoped, this publication will be of help to researchers working on any aspect of ancient Mathura in particular and on Indian art and culture in general. For any shortcomings in the book, the responsibility is entirely mine.

25 March 1991

Jagdish S. Yadav
Editor

ACKNOWLEDGEMENTS

Dr. Pradeep Mehendiratta, Director, American Institute of Indian Studies suggested to me the idea of compiling this bibliography. I am most grateful to him for his suggestion, support, encouragement and also for writing the Foreword. Thanks are due to Prof. Susan Huntington and Prof. Catherine B. Asher for their sustained support. I am thankful to Dr. N.P. Joshi for his valuable suggestions. I would like to record my great appreciation and thanks to my colleague Mr. O.N. Pandey without his cooperation it would not have been possible to complete this work. Mr. V.K. Venkatavaradhan and Mr. V.K. Gupta typed the manuscript in a very short time for which I am grateful to them. I record my sincere thanks to Mr. Ramesh Jain of Manohar for his valuable suggestions in the publication of this work. My wife Nirmala assisted me in compilation of the bibliography, I am grateful to her and our son Yogesh and daughter Shikha.

Jagdish S. Yadav

CLASSIFIED SUBJECT INDEX

HISTORICAL BACKGROUND

1. **Agrawala, V.S.**
Bodha Sahitya me Shoorsen janapad. In Radhey Shyam Dwivedi, ed., *Braj Vaibhav*. Mathura, Bharati Anusandhan Bhawan, 1972: 71-72. (Hindi)

2. _____.
Itihasa-darsana. Varanasi, Prithivi Prakashan, 1978. (Hindi)

3. _____.
Katra Keshavdev. In Thakur Prasad Verma and others, ed., *Yugayugina Vraja*. Varanasi, Bharatiya Itihasa Samkalan Samiti, U.P., 1988: 69-77.

4. _____.
The seven-sea gift in the Matsya Purana. *Purana*, Vol. 1, No. 2, February 1960: 206-212.

5. _____.
Shri Krishna: Janamabhumi ya Katra Keshavdev. In V.S. Agrawala, ed., *Seth Kanhaiya Lal Poddar abhinandana grantha*. Mathura, Akhila Bharatiya Braj Sahitya Mandal, 1953: 745-752. (Hindi)

6. **Bajpai, K.D.**
Govardhana. *Vallabh Vidyanagar Research Bulletin*, Vol. 1, No. 1, 1957: 11-12. (Hindi)

7. _____.
Mathura. New Delhi, McMillan Company of India, 1980.

8. _____.
Mathura-parichaya. Mathura, Lok Sahitya Sahyogi Prakashan, 1950. (Hindi)

9. _____.
Some problems of ancient Indian history. *Bulletin of Ancient Indian History and Archaeology*, No. 1, 1967: 1-6.

10. _____.
Videshi lekhakon ka Braj varnan-2. In Radhey Shyam Dwivedi, ed., *Braj Vaibhav*. Mathura, Bharati Anusandhan Bhawan, 1972: 85-88. (Hindi)

11. _____.
Videshi lekhakon ka Mathura varnan. In Radhey Shyam Dwivedi, ed., *Braj Vaibhav*. Mathura, Bharati Anusandhan Bhawan, 1972: 73-78. (Hindi)

12. _____.
Videshi lekhakon ka Mathura varnan. In V.S. Agrawala, ed., *Seth Kanhaiya Lal Poddar abhinandana grantha*. Mathura, Akhila Bharatiya Braj Sahitya Mandal, 1953: 827-837. (Hindi)

13. **Banerji, R.D.**
Age of the imperial Guptas. New Delhi, Ramanand Vidya Bhawan, 1981.

14. **Basham, A.L.**, ed.
Papers on the date of Kaniska submitted to the conference on the date of Kaniska, London, 20-22 April, 1960. Leiden, E.J. Brill, 1968.

15. **Bhandarkar, D.R.**
Foreign elements in the Hindu population. *Indian Antiquary*, Vol. 40, No. 1, January 1911: 7-37.

16. _____.
Foreign elements in the Hindu population. *Journal of Ancient Indian History*, Vol. 1, 1967-68: 267-328.

17. **Bhandarkar, R.G.**
A peep into the early history of India from the foundation of the Maurya dynasty to the fall of the Imperial Gupta dynasty (B.C. 322-Circa 500 A.D.) *Journal of the Bombay Branch of the Royal Asiatic Society*, Vol. 20, 1897-1900: 356-408.

18. **Bongard-Levin, G.M.**
Ancient Indian civilization. New Delhi, Arnold-Heinemann, 1985.

19. **Bussagli, M.**
The Problem of Kaniska as seen by the art historian. In A.L. Basham, ed., *Papers on the date of Kaniska*. Leiden, E.J. Brill, 1968: 39-56.

20. Cambridge History of India, Vol. 1: Ancient India, edited by E.J. Rapson. Delhi, S. Chand & Co., 1962.

21. **Chakladar, H.C.**
The Geography of Kalidasa. Calcutta, Indian Studies: Past & Present, 1963.

22. **Chandorkar, Ashok**
Vraja-yatra. In Thakur Prasad Verma and others, ed., *Yugayugina Vraja.* Varanasi, Bharatiya Itihasa Samkalana Samiti, U.P., 1988: 45-48. (Hindi)

23. **Chatterjee, Asim Kumar**
Historicity of Vasudeva Krsna. In A.M. Shastri and others, ed., *Vajapeya: Essays on evolution of Indian art & culture; Prof. K.D. Bajpai felicitation volume,* Vol. 2. Delhi, Agam Kala Prakashan, 1987: 389-392.

24. **Chattopadhyaya, B.D.**
Mathura from the Sunga to the Kusana period: An historical outline. In Doris Meth Srinivasan, ed., *Mathura: The cultural heritage.* New Delhi, American Institute of Indian Studies, 1989: 19-28.

25. **Chattopadhyaya, Sudhakar**
Early history of north India from the fall of the Mauryas to the death of Harsa, C. 200 B.C.-A.D. 650. Calcutta, Progressive Publishers, 1958.

26. **Chaturvedi, Bal Mukund**
Braj bhumi ke pracheen darshniya devata aur sthan. In Radhey Shyam Dwivedi, ed., *Braj Vaibhav.* Mathura, Bharati Anusandhan Bhawan, 1972: 263- 268. (Hindi)

27. _____.
Mahabharat me Braj. In Radhey Shyam Dwivedi, ed., *Braj Vaibhav.* Mathura, Bharati Anusandhan Bhawan, 1972: 55-60. (Hindi)

28. _____.
Purano me Braj. In Radhey Shyam Dwivedi, ed., *Braj Vaibhav.* Mathura, Bharati Anusandhan Bhawan, 1972: 21-28. (Hindi)

29. _____.
Valmiki Ramayana me Braj. In Radhey Shyam Dwivedi, ed., *Braj Vaibhav.* Mathura, Bharati Anusandhan Bhawan, 1972: 29-34. (Hindi)

30. _____.
Vedo me Braj. In Radhey Shyam Dwivedi, ed., *Braj Vaibhav*. Mathura, Bharati Anusandhan Bhawan, 1972: 13-20. (Hindi)

31. **Chaturvedi, Sarojini**
Foreign influx and interaction with Indian culture. Delhi, Agam Kala Prakashan, 1985.

32. **Chaturvedi, Vasudev Krisna**
Braj sushma Sri Yamuna. In Radhey Shyam Dwivedi, ed., *Braj Vaibhav*. Mathura, Bharati Anusandhan Bhawan, 1972: 49-54. (Hindi)

33. **Chaturvedi, Vitthal Sharma**
Braj ka adhyatimik swaroop. In Radhey Shyam Dwivedi, ed., *Braj Vaibhav*. Mathura, Bharati Anusandhan Bhawan, 1972: 10-12. (Hindi)

34. Chronology. *Marg*. Vol. 15, No. 2, March 1962: 4.

35. Comprehensive History of India. New Delhi, Indian History Congress. Vol. 2: Mauryas & Satavahanas, edited by K.A. Nilakanta Sastri, 325 B.C. - A.D. 300, 1957. Vol. 3: A.D. 300-985, edited by R.C. Majumdar and K.K. Dasgupta, 1982.

36. **Cunningham, A.**
Ancient geography of India. Varanasi, Indological Book House, 1963.

37. **Dalal, Roshan**
The Historical geography of the Mathura region. In Doris Meth Srinivasan, ed., *Mathura: The cultural heritage*. New Delhi, American Institute of Indian Studies, 1989: 3-11.

38. **Dandekar, R.N.**
The Age of the Guptas and other essays. Delhi, Ajanta Publications, 1982.

39. **Dani, A.H.**
The Date of Kaniska. In A.L. Basham, ed., *Papers on the date of Kaniska*. Leiden, E.J. Brill, 1968: 57-66.

40. **Dey, Nundo Lal**
The Geographical dictionary of ancient and mediaeval India. New Delhi, Oriental Books Reprint Corporation, 1971.

41. **Dixit, Uma Shankar**
Giri Govardhan aur uska anchal. In Radhey Shyam Dwivedi, ed., *Braj Vaibhav*. Mathura, Bharati Anusandhan Bhawan, 1972: 280-285. (Hindi)

42. _____.
Nandgaon—Barsana. In Radhey Shyam Dwivedi, ed., *Braj Vaibhav*. Mathura, Bharati Anusandhan Bhawan, 1972: 276-277. (Hindi)

43. **Drake-Brockman, D.L.**, ed.
Muttra: A gazetteer. Allahabad, Government Press, 1911.

44. **Dwivedi, Radhey Shyam**
Braj ke van aur upavan. In Radhey Shyam Dwivedi, ed., *Braj Vaibhav*. Mathura, Bharati Anusandhan Bhawan, 1972: 291-296. (Hindi)

45. _____.
Braj ki pracheenata aur mahatta. In Radhey Shyam Dwivedi, ed., *Braj Vaibhav*. Mathura, Bharati Anusandhan Bhawan, 1972: 1-5. (Hindi)

46. _____.
Braj rajdhani Madhupuri kinva Mathura (Purana kaal). In Radhey Shyam Dwivedi, ed., *Braj Vaibhav*. Mathura, Bharati Anusandhan Bhawan, 1972: 41-48. (Hindi)

47. _____.
Braj van yatra ke visram sthal. In Radhey Shyam Dwivedi, ed., *Braj Vaibhav*. Mathura, Bharati Anusandhan Bhawan, 1972: 307-308. (Hindi)

48. _____.
Brajdham aur Golok. In Radhey Shyam Dwivedi, ed., *Braj Vaibhav*. Mathura, Bharati Anusandhan Bhawan, 1972: 6-9. (Hindi)

49. **Fergusson, James**
On the Saka, Samvat and Gupta eras. *Journal of the Royal Asiatic Society of Great Britain and Ireland*, New Series, Vol. 12, 1880: 259-85.

50. **Ganguly, D.K.**
The imperial Guptas and their times. New Delhi, Abhinav Publications, 1987.

51. **Gokhale, B.G.**
Samudra Gupta; life and times. Bombay, Asia Publishing House, 1962.

52. **Goyal, S.R.**
A history of the imperial Guptas. Allahabad, Central Book Depot, 1967.

53. **Growse, F.S.**
The country of Braj. *Journal of the Asiatic Society of Bengal,* Vol. 40, pt. 1, No. 1, 1871: 34-45.

54. _____.
Mathura: A district memoir. Second edition. Government Press, 1880.

55. _____.
Mathura notes. *Journal of the Asiatic Society of Bengal,* Vol. 47, pt. 1, No. 2, 1878: 97-133.

56. _____.
Sketches of Mathura: The Ban yatra. *Indian Antiquary*, Vol. 1, 1872: 133-137.

57. _____.
Sketches of Mathura: Barsana and Nandgaon. *Indian Antiquary,* Vol. 1, 1872: 311-314

58. _____.
Sketches of Mathura : The Braj Mandal. *Indian Antiquary,* Vol. 1, 1872: 65-69.

59. _____.
Sketches of Mathura: Gobardhan. *Indian Antiquary*, Vol. 1, 1872: 230-234.

60. _____.
The tirthas of Vrindavana and Gokula. *Journal of the Asiatic Society,* Vol. 41, pt. 1, No. 4, 1872: 313-331.

61. **Gupta, Parmanand**
Geographical names in ancient Indian inscriptions. Delhi, Concept Publishing Company, 1977.

62. _____.
Geography in ancient Indian inscriptions (up to 650 A.D.). Delhi, D.K. Publishing House, 1973.

63. **Gupta, P.L.**
Gupta samrajya. Varanasi, Vishwavidyalaya Prakashan, 1970. (Hindi)

64. _____.
The imperial Guptas. Varanasi, Vishwavidyalaya Prakashan, 1974-79. 2 Vols.

65. **Hein, Norvin**
Kalayavana, a key to Mathura's cultural self-perception. In Doris Meth Srinivasan, ed., *Mathura: The cultural heritage.* New Delhi, American Institute of Indian Studies, 1989: 223-235.

66. **Hewitt, J.F.**
Notes on the early history of Northern India. *Journal of the Royal Asiatic Society of Great Britain and Ireland*, New Series, Vol. 21, 1889: 187-359.

67. **Indarji, Bhagvanlal**
The northern Kshatrapas. *Journal of the Royal Asiatic Society of Great Britain and Ireland*, 1894: 541-554.

68. _____.
The Western Kshatrapas. *Journal of the Royal Asiatic Society of Great Britain and Ireland,* 1890: 639-62.

69. **Jain, Jagdish Chandra**
Pracheen Jain-sahitya me Mathura. In Vasudeva Sharan Agrawala, ed., *Seth Kanhaiya Lal Poddar abhinandana grantha.* Mathura, Akhila Bharatiya Braj Sahitya Mandal, 1953: 823-826.(Hindi)

70. **Jain, Jyoti Prasad**
The Jaina sources of the history of ancient India (100 B.C.-A.D. 900). Delhi, Munshiram Manoharlal, 1964.

71. _____.
Mathura. *Jaina Siddhanta Bhaskar,* Vol. 22, No. 2, December 1955: 23-32. (Hindi)

72. **Jayaswal, K.P.**
Problems of Saka-Satavahana history. *Journal of the Bihar and Orissa Research Society,* Vol. 16, pts. 3-4, September-December 1930: 227-316.

73. _____.
The statue of Wema Kadphises and Kushan chronology. *Journal of the Bihar and Orissa Research Society*, Vol. 6, pt. 1, March 1920: 12-22.

74. **Joshi, Narendra Prakash**
New light on the Gupta era and the chronology of early Gupta kings. *Vishveshvaranand Indological Journal*, Vol. 14, 1976: 245-260.

75. **Kailash Chandra**
Mahavan aur Ramanreti. In Radhey Shyam Dwivedi, ed., *Braj Vaibhav*. Mathura, Bharati Anusandhan Bhawan, 1972: 278-279. (Hindi)

76. **Kameshwar Prasad**
Factors influencing the growth of towns in the Kusana period. *Journal of the Bihar Research Society*, Vol. 62, 1976: 73-80.

77. _____.
Town planning and structures in the Kusana period. *Journal of the Bihar Research Society*, Vols. 63-64, 1977-1978: 100-139.

78. **Krishnacharya**
Vikramaditya ke samay me Braj. In Radhey Shyam Dwivedi, ed., *Braj Vaibhav*. Mathura, Bharati Anusandhan Bhawan, 1972: 61-64. (Hindi)

79. **Lahiri, Bela**
Indigenous states of northern India (circa 200 B.C. to 320 A.D.). Calcutta, University of Calcutta, 1974.

80. **Law, B.C.**
Geographical aspect of Kalidasa's works. Calcutta, Indian Research Institute, 1954.

81. _____.
Geography of early Buddhism. London, Kegan Paul, Trench, Trubner & Co., 1932.

82. _____.
Historical geography of ancient India. Paris, Societe Asiatique de Paris, 1954.

83. _____.
Mathura: An ancient Indian city. *Quarterly Journal of the Mythic Society*, Vol. 32, No. 1, July 1941: 1-7.

84. _____.
Mathura in ancient India. *Journal of the Royal Asiatic Society of Bengal, Letters*, Vol. 13, No. 1, 1947: 21-30.

85. **Maity, Sachindra Kumar**
The imperial Guptas and their times. New Delhi, Munshiram Manoharlal, 1975.

86. **Majumdar, R.C.**
The date of Kaniska. In A.L. Basham, ed., *Papers on the date of Kaniska.* Leiden, E.J. Brill, 1968: 150-154.

87. _____.
The history and culture of the Indian people. Bombay, Bharatiya Vidya Bhavan. Vol. 2: The age of imperial unity. 1951. Vol. 3: The classical age, 1954.

88. _____.
North India after the fall of the Maurya empire. *Journal of the Numismatic Society of India*, Vol. 22, 1960: 47-55.

89. **Marshall, J.H**
The date of Kanishka. *Journal of the Royal Asiatic Society of Great Britain and Ireland*, 1914: 973-986.

90. **Mathur, Vijayendra Kumar**
Etihasik sthanavali. New Delhi, Shiksha Mantralaya, 1969. (Hindi)

91. Mathura of the Gods. *Marg*, Vol. 15, No. 2, March 1962: 2-3.

92. **Misra, Bhaskarnath**
Ashtadasha purano me Mathura. In Vasudeva Sharan Agrawala, ed., *Seth Kanhaiya Lal Poddar abhinandana grantha.* Mathura, Akhila Bharatiya Braj Sahitya Mandal, 1953: 803-819. (Hindi)

93. **Mookerji, Radha Kumud**
The Gupta empire. Delhi, Motilal Banarsidass, 1969.

94. **Mukherjee, B.N.**
Disintegration of the Kushana empire. Varanasi, Banaras Hindu University, 1976.

95. _____.
The Kushana genealogy. Calcutta, Sanskrit College, 1967.

96. _____.
Mathura and its society: The Saka-Pahlava phase. Calcutta, Firma K.L.M. Private Limited, 1981.

97. _____.
The rise and fall of the Kushana empire. Calcutta, Firma K.L.M Private Limited, 1988.

98. **Narain, A.K.**
The date of Kaniska. In A.L. Basham, ed., *Papers on the date of Kaniska*. Leiden, E.J. Brill, 1968: 206-239.

99. **Pathak, Visnu Chandra**
Jat Maratha sangharsa aur Braj. In Radhey Shyam Dwivedi, ed., *Braj Vaibhav*. Mathura, Bharati Anusandhan Bhawan, 1972: 156-162. (Hindi)

100. **Prakash, Vidya** and **Roy, T.N.**
Sites and monuments of Uttar Pradesh. *Bulletin of the U.P. Historical Society*, No. 4, 1965: 1-56.

101. **Puri, B.N.**
India under the Kushanas. Bombay, Bharatiya Vidya Bhavan, 1965.

102. **Puri, B.**
The later Kushans. In *Central Asia in the Kushan period: Proceedings of the International Conference of the History, Archaeology and Culture of Central Asia in the Kushan period*, 1968, Vol. 2. UNESCO, 1975: 56-65.

103. **Ray Chaudhuri, Hemchandra**
Political history of ancient India. Calcutta, University of Calcutta, 1953.

104. **Roy, Ashim Kumar** and **Gidwani, N.N.**
A dictionary of Indology. New Delhi, Oxford & IBH Publishing Co., 1985. Vol. 3.

105. **Roy, Udai Narain**
Gupta-rajvansha tatha uska yug. Allahabad, Lokbharati Prakashan, 1977. (Hindi)

106. **Saletore, R.N.**
Encyclopaedia of Indian culture. New Delhi, Sterling Publishers, 1983. Vol. 3.

107. **Satyendra, Satyanarain**
Yavanakaal aur Braj. In Radhey Shyam Dwivedi, ed., *Braj Vaibhav*. Mathura, Bharati Anusandhan Bhawan, 1972: 89-104. (Hindi)

108. **Sharma, Brahmanand**
Yuga-yugin Vraja. In Thakur Prasad Verma and others, ed., *Yugayugina Vraja.* Varanasi, Bharatiya Itihasa Samkalana Samiti, U.P., 1988: 26-28. (Hindi)

109. **Sharma, G.R.**, ed.
Kusana studies. Allahabad, University of Allahabad, 1968.

110. **Sharma, Govind**
Vrandavan ke pracheen ullekha aur naamkaran. In Thakur Prasad Verma and others, ed., *Yugayugina Vraja.* Varanasi, Bharatiya Itihasa Samkalana Samiti, U.P., 1988: 29-32. (Hindi)

111. **Sharma, Hitsharan,** ed.
Sri Krsna janmasthan smarika. Mathura, Sri Krsna Janmasthan Sevasthan, 1982. (Hindi)

112. **Sharma, Mohan Lal**
Karhala -jahan te raas prakat bhayo. In Radhey Shyam Dwivedi, ed., *Braj Vaibhav.* Mathura, Bharati Anusandhan Bhawan, 1972: 286-288. (Hindi)

113. **Sharma, Pinak Pani Prasad**
Teerthas in the Narada Puran. *Journal of the Gujarat Research Society,* Vol. 36, No. 4, October 1974: 21-26.

114. **Sharma, Ramesh Chandra**
Mathura ka Jaina tirtha-Kankali. Mathura, D. Jaina Siddha Kshetra Prabandh Samiti, 1971. (Hindi)

115. **Shukla, Govardhan Nath**
Skanda puran me Braj. In Radhey Shyam Dwivedi, ed., *Braj Vaibhav.* Mathura, Bharati Anusandhan Bhawan, 1972: 37-40. (Hindi)

116. **Singh, M.R.**
Geographical data in the early puranas—a critical study. Calcutta, Punthi Pustak, 1972.

117. **Singh, Rana P.B.** and **Dubey, D.P.**
Mathura Mandala: Territory and sacrality. In Thakur Prasad Verma and others, ed., *Yugayugina Vraja.* Varanasi, Bharatiya Itihasa Samkalan Samiti, U.P., 1988: 189-200.

118. **Sircar, D.C.**
The account of the Yavanas in the Yuga-purana. *Journal of the Royal Asiatic Society of Great Britain and Ireland,* 1963: 7-20.

119. ____.
A note on the date of the Satraps of Mathura. *Indian Historical Quarterly,* Vol. 24, No. 3, September 1948: 242-243.

120. ____.
Some problems concerning the Kusanas. Dharwar, Kannada Research Institute, 1971.

121. ____.
The Yavanas and Mathura. *Journal of Ancient Indian History,* Vol. 6, pts. 1-2, 1972-73: 168-173.

122. **Smith, Vincent A.**
The Kushan, or Indo-Scythian period of Indian history B.C. 165 to A.D. 320. *Journal of the Royal Asiatic Society of Great Britain and Ireland*, 1903: 1-64.

123. **Srinivasan, Doris Meth,** ed.
Mathura: The cultural heritage. New Delhi, American Institute of Indian Studies, 1989.

124. **Sykes, W.H.**
Notes on the religious, moral and political state of India before the Mahomedan invasion, chiefly founded on the travels of the Chinese Buddhist priest Fa Hian in India, A.D. 399, and on the commentaries of Messrs. Remusat, Klaproth, Burnouf, and Landresse. *Journal of the Royal Asiatic Society of Great Britain and Ireland,* Vol. 6, 1841: 248-484.

125. **Tandon, Malathi**
Madhuvana. *Studies in Indian Place Names,* Vol. 3: 82-83.

126. **Thakur, Umakant**
Holy places of North India. *Purana*, Vol. 15, No. 2, July 1973: 201-222.

127. **Thakur, Vijay Kumar**
Urbanisation in ancient India. New Delhi, Abhinav Publications, 1981.

128. **Thapar, B.**
The Kushan civilisation in India: An appraisal of the component elements. In *Central Asia in the Kushan period: Proceedings of the International Conference on the History, Archaeology and Culture of Central Asia in the Kushan period,* 1968, Vol. 1, UNESCO, 1974: 90-94.

129. **Thapar, Romila**
The early history of Mathura: Up to and including the Mauryan period. In Doris Meth Srinivasan, ed., *Mathura: The cultural heritage.* New Delhi, American Institute of Indian Studies, 1989: 12-18.

130. **Thomas, E.**
The early faith of Asoka. *Journal of the Royal Asiatic Society of Great Britain and Ireland,* New Series, Vol. 9, 1877: 155-234.

131. **Thomas, F.W.**
The date of Kaniska. *Journal of the Royal Asiatic Society of Great Britain and Ireland,* 1913: 627-650.

132. **Upadhyaya, Bharat Singh**
Buddha kalin Bharatiya bhugol. Prayag, Hindi Sahitya Sammelan, 1961. (Hindi)

133. Uttar Pradesh District Gazetteers: Mathura. Lucknow, Government of Uttar Pradesh, 1968.

134. **Verma, Thakur Prasad** and others, ed.
Yugayugin Vraja. Varanasi, Bharatiya Itihasa Samkalan Samiti, U.P., 1988.

135. **Vidya Prakash** and **Roy, T.N.**
Sites and monuments of Uttar Pradesh. *Journal of U.P. Historical Society,* New Series, Vol. 11-13, pt. 2: 119-174.

136. **Vrindavan Das**
Jato ka shasan kaal aur Braj. In Radhey Shyam Dwivedi, ed., *Braj Vaibhav.* Mathura, Bharati Anusandhan Bhawan, 1972: 149-155. (Hindi)

137. **Yajnavakya, Satyendu**
Ahmadshah Abdali dwara Vraja-Vidhvansa aur narsanhaar. In Thakur Prasad Verma and others, ed. *Yugayugina Vraja*. Varanasi, Bharatiya Itihasa Smkalan Samiti, U.P., 1988: 56-58. (Hindi)

SOCIETY AND ECONOMY

138. **Agrawal, Rajendra Kumar**
Braj ka vaibhavshali pashu chikitsa mahavidyalaya (Bantnari College). In Radhey Shyam Dwivedi, ed., *Braj Vaibhav*. Mathura, Bharati Anusandhan Bhawan, 1972: 289-290. (Hindi)

139. **Agrawala, V.S.,** ed.
Seth Kanhaiya Lal Poddar adhinandana grantha. Mathura, Akhila Bharatiya Braj Sahitya Mandal, 1953. (Hindi)

140. **Bajpai, Shiva G.**
Mathura: Trade routes, commerce, and communication patterns, from the post-Mauryan period to the end of the Kusana period. In Doris Meth Srinivasan, ed., *Mathura: The cultural heritage*. New Delhi, American Institute of Indian Studies, 1989: 46-58.

141. **Chakraberti, Kanchan**
Society, religion and art of the Kushan India: A historico-symbiosis. Calcutta, K.P. Bagchi & Co., 1981.

142. **Chaturvedi, Balmukund**
Braj me malla vidya. In Radhey Shyam Dwivedi, ed., *Braj Vaibhav*. Mathura, Bharati Anusandhan Bhawan, 1972: 217-220. (Hindi)

143. **Chaturvedi,Vitthal Sharma**
Braj ki sanskriti. In Radhey Shyam Dwivedi, ed., *Braj Vaibhav*. Mathura, Bharati Anusandhan Bhawan, 1972: 225-236. (Hindi)

144. **Dwivedi, Radhey Shyam**
Braj ke mele va phool dol. In Radhey Shyam Dwivedi, ed., *Braj Vaibhav*. Mathura, Bharati Anusandhan Bhawan, 1972: 313-314. (Hindi)

145. _____.
Braj sanskriti. In Radhey Shyam Dwivedi, ed., *Braj Vaibhav*. Mathura, Bharati Anusandhan Bhawan, 1972: 237. (Hindi)

146. _____.
Go sanvardhini Braj sanskriti. In Radhey Shyam Dwivedi, ed., *Braj Vaibhav*. Mathura, Bharati Anusandhan Bhawan, 1972: 223-224. (Hindi)

147. **Gafurov, G.**
Kushan civilisation and world culture. *Indian Studies: Past and Present*, Vol. 11, No. 1, October-December 1969: 1-14.

148. **Growse, F.S.**
The etymology of local names in Northern India, as exemplified in the district of Maṭhura. *Journal of the Asiatic Society of Bengal*, Vol. 43, pt. 1, No. 4, 1874: 324- 356.

149. **Haridutt Shastri**
Braj sanskriti aur lok sanskriti. In Radhey Shyam Dwivedi, ed., *Braj Vaibhav*. Mathura, Bharati Anusandhan Bhawan, 1972: 238-240. (Hindi)

150. **Joshi, N.P.**
Life in ancient Uttarpatha. Lucknow, The author, 1967.

151. **Kameshwar Parsad**
Cities, crafts and commerce under the Kusanas. Delhi, Agam Kala Prakashan, 1984.

152. **Lohuizen-de Leeuw, J.E. van**
Foreign elements in Indian culture introduced during the Scythian period with special reference to Mathura. In Doris Meth Srinivasan, ed., *Mathura: The cultural heritage*. New Delhi, American Institute of Indian Studies, 1989: 72-82.

153. **Mittal, Prabhu Dayal**
Braj ka sanskritika itihasa. Delhi, Rajkamal Prakashan, 1966. (Hindi)

154. _____.
Braj ke dharma-sampradayon ka itihasa. Delhi, National Publishing House, 1968. (Hindi)

155. _____.
Braj ke utsava, tyohar aur mele. Mathura, Sahitya Sansthan, 1966. (Hindi)

156. ____.
Braj ki sanskritik yatra. Mathura, Sahitya Sansthan, 1966. (Hindi)

157. **Moti Chandra**
Costumes, textiles, cosmetics & coiffure in ancient and mediaeval India. Delhi, Oriental Publishers, 1973.

158. **Mukherjee, B.N.**
Growth of Mathura and its society (up to the end of the Kusana age). In Doris Meth Srinivasan, ed., *Mathura: The cultural heritage*. New Delhi, American Institute of Indian Studies, 1989: 59-71.

159. **Mukhiya, Nanalal**
Braj ke hindola utsava. In Radhey Shyam Dwivedi, ed., *Braj Vaibhav*. Mathura, Bharati Anusandhan Bhawan, 1972: 309-312. (Hindi)

160. **Pandey, Indu Prabha**
Dress and ornaments in ancient India. Delhi, Bharatiya Vidya Prakashan, 1988.

161. **Parikh, Dwaraka Das**
Braj yatra aur uska prachalan. In Radhey Shyam Dwivedi, ed., *Braj Vaibhav*. Mathura, Bharati Anusandhan Bhawan, 1972: 301-307. (Hindi)

162. **Pathak, Haldhar**
Cultural history of the Gupta period based on epigraphic and numismatic records. Delhi, Bharatiya Publishing House, 1978.

163. **Puri, B.N.**
Some aspects of economic life in the Kusana period. *Indian Culture*, Vol. 12, No. 2, October-December 1945: 82-87.

164. ____.
Some aspects of social life in Kusana period. *Indian Culture*, Vol. 16, No. 1, July-September 1949: 49-57.

165. **Ranchoda Acharya**
Braj sanskriti vedic sanskriti hai. In Radhey Shyam Dwivedi, ed., *Braj Vaibhav*. Mathura, Bharati Anusandhan Bhawan, 1972: 221-222. (Hindi)

166. **Saletore, Rajaram Narayan**
Life in the Gupta age. Bombay, The Popular Book Depot. 1943.

167. **Salomon, Richard**
Daily life in ancient Mathura. In Doris Meth Srinivasan, ed., *Mathura: The cultural heritage.* New Delhi, American Institute of Indian Studies, 1989: 39-45.

168. **Sharma, R.S.**
Trends in the economic history of Mathura (c. 300 B.C. - A.D. 300). *Indological Taurinensia,* Vols. 8-9, 1980-81: 415-427.

169. _____.
Trends in the economic history of Mathura (c. 300 B.C.-A.D. 300). In Doris Meth Srinivasan, ed., *Mathura: The cultural heritage.* New Delhi, American Institute of Indian Studies, 1989: 31-38.

170. **Tiwari, Balji**
Braj yatra ki parampara. In Radhey Shyam Dwivedi, ed., *Braj Vaibhav.* Mathura, Bharati Anusandhan Bhawan, 1972: 297-300. (Hindi)

171. **Vijay Nath**
Dana in the context of commerce and urbanisation in Kusana times. *Journal of the Bihar Research Society,* Vols. 65-66, 1979-80: 166-177.

172. **Wayamn, Alex**
The Mathura set of astamangala (eight auspicious symbols) in early and later times. In Doris Meth Srinivasan, ed., *Mathura: The cultural heritage.* New Delhi, American Institute of Indian Studies, 1989: 236-246.

RELIGIOUS SECTS

HINDU

173. **Agrawal, Radhey Shyam**
Braj aur Vaisnava Acarya. In Radhey Shyam Dwivedi, ed., *Braj Vaibhav*. Mathura, Bharati Anusandhan Bhawan, 1972: 146. (Hindi)

174. **Bhayani, H.C.**
The childhood exploits of Krsna. *Sambodhi*, Vol. 11, 1982-1983: 121-132.

175. **Chanda, Ramaprasad**
Archaeology and Vaishnava tradition. *Indian Museum Bulletin*, Vol. 13, 1978: 45-62.

176. _____.
Archaeology and Vaishnava tradition. Calcutta, Government Printing, 1920. (Memoirs of the Archaeological Survey of India No. 5).

177. **Dhakad, Giriraj Prasad**
Vraja me shakti upasana ka prarambha aur vikas. In Thakur Prasad Verma and others, ed., *Yugayugina Vraja*. Varanasi, Bharatiya Itihasa Samkalan Samiti, U.P., 1988: 65-68. (Hindi)

178. **Dwivedi, Radhey Shyam**
Braj aur anya Vaisnava-sampradaya. In Radhey Shyam Dwivedi, ed., *Braj Vaibhav*. Mathura, Bharati Anusandhan Bhawan, 1972 : 147-148. (Hindi)

179. _____.
Braj aur Shaiva dharm. In Radhey Shyam Dwivedi, ed., *Braj Vaibhav*. Mathura, Bharati Anusandhan Bhawan, 1972: 113-115. (Hindi)

180. **Goswami, Kunja Gobinda**
Saivism in Saka-Kusana period. *Journal of the Asiatic Society*, Vol. 27, No. 2, 1985: 45-57.

181. **Hartel, Herbert**
Aspects of early Naga cult in India. *Journal of the Royal Society of Arts,* October 1976: 663-683.

182. **Hiltebeitel, Alf.**
Krsna at Mathura. In Doris Meth Srinivasan, ed., *Mathura: The cultural heritage.* New Delhi, American Institute of Indian Studies, 1989: 93-102.

183. **Kennedy, J.**
The child Krishna, Christianity and the Gujars. *Journal of the Royal Asiatic Society of Great Britain and Ireland,* 1907: 951-991.

184. **Madhav Rai**
Braj sahitya ko pustimarg ki den. In Radhey Shyam Dwivedi, ed., *Braj Vaibhav.* Mathura, Bharati Anusandhan Bhawan, 1972: 134-136. (Hindi)

185. **Malarvindam**
Braj sanskriti aur Vallabh sampradaya. In Radhey Shyam Dwivedi, ed., *Braj Vaibhav.* Mathura, Bharati Anusandhan Bhawan, 1972: 137-140. (Hindi)

186. **Mittal, Prabhu Dayal**
Brajastha Vallabh sampradaya ka itihas. Mathura, Sahitya Sansthan, 1968. (Hindi)

187. _____.
Chaitanya mat aur Braj sahitya. Mathura, Sahitya Sansthan, 1962. (Hindi)

188. **Rajendra Ranjan**
Braj aur Vallabh sampradaya. In Radhey Shyam Dwivedi, ed., *Braj Vaibhav.* Mathura, Bharati Anusandhan Bhawan, 1972: 141-142. (Hindi)

189. _____.
Braj me shakti upasana. In Radhey Shyam Dwivedi, ed., *Braj Vaibhav.* Mathura, Bharati Anusandhan Bhawan, 1972: 105-112. (Hindi)

190. **Sarkar, Amal**
Krishna and the Krishna cult. *Indian Museum Bulletin,* Vol. 11, No. 2, July 1976: 59-62.

191. **Sharma, Shyam**
Sri Chaitanya sampradaya aur Braj. In Radhey Shyam Dwivedi, ed., *Braj Vaibhav*. Mathura, Bharati Anusandhan Bhawan, 1972: 125-133. (Hindi)

192. **Sharma, Ved Prakash**
Braj aur Shuk sampradaya. In Radhey Shyam Dwivedi, ed., *Braj Vaibhav*. Mathura, Bharati Anusandhan Bhawan, 1972: 143-145. (Hindi)

193. **Singh, R.C.**
Worship of Vasudeva-Krsna in ancient India based on archaeological evidences. *Bulletin of Museums & Archaeology in U.P.*, Nos. 21-24; June 1978- December 1979: 37-42.

194. **Srivastava, V.C.**
The Kusanas and the Sun cult. *Journal of the Ganganatha Jha Kendriya Sanskrit Vidyapeetha*, Vol. 35, pts. 3-4, July-December 1979: 115-146.

195. **Vogel, J. Ph.**
Naga worship in ancient Mathura. *Archaeological Survey of India Annual Report*, 1908-09: 158-163.

196. **Vrajavallabh Sharan**
Sri Nimbark sampradaya aur Braj. In Radhey Shyam Dwivedi, ed., *Braj Vaibhav*. Mathura, Bharati Anusandhan Bhawan, 1972: 116-123. (Hindi)

BUDDHIST

197. **Bajpai, K.D.**
Some recent discoveries and their bearing on Buddhism. *Bulletin of Museums and Archaeology in U.P.*, Nos 41-42, June-December 1988: 87-91.

198. **Bapat, P.V.**
2500 years of Buddhism. New Delhi, Publications Division, 1956.

199. **Bhattacharyya, B.**
The Buddhist pantheon and its classification. In *Commemorative essays presented to Professor Kashinath Bapuji Pathak*. Poona, Bhandarkar Oriental Research Institute, 1934: 80-93.

200. **Datta Nalinaksha**
The Mahasanghika School of Buddhism. *Journal of the Department of Letters,* Vol. 8: 117-129.

201. **Dutt, Nalinaksha and Bajpai, K.D.**
Development of Buddhism in Uttar Pradesh. Lucknow, Publication Bureau, Government of U.P., 1956.

202. **Huntington, John C.**
Mathura evidence for the early teachings of Mahayana. In Doris Meth Srinivasan, ed., *Mathura: The cultural heritage.* New Delhi, American Institute of Indian Studies, 1989: 85-92.

203. **Jaini, Padmanabh S.**
Political and cultural data in references to Mathura in the Buddhist literature. In Doris Meth Srinivasan, ed., *Mathura: The cultural heritage.* New Delhi. American Institute of Indian Studies, 1989: 214-222.

204. **Khosla, Sarla**
The historical evolution of the Buddha legend. New Delhi, Intellectual Publishing House, 1989.

205. **Margabandhu, C.**
Archaeological evidence of Buddhism at Mathura—a chronological study. In K.V. Ramesh and others, ed., *Svasti Sri: B.Ch. Chhabra felicitation volume.* Delhi, Agam Kala Prakashan, 1984: 267-279.

206. **Misra, Satish Chandra**
Bodh dharma aur Braj. In Radhey Shyam Dwivedi, ed., *Braj Vaibhav.* Mathura, Bharati Anusandhan Bhawan, 1972: 65-70. (Hindi)

207. **Przyluski, Jean**
Fables in the Vinaya-pitaka of the Sarvastivadin School. *Indian Historical Quarterly,* Vol. 5, No. 1, March 1929: 1-5.

208. **Schopen, Gregory**
On monks, nuns and 'vulgar' practices: The introduction to the image cult into Indian Buddhism. *Artibus Asiae,* Vol. 49, Nos. 1-2, 1988-1989: 153-168.

209. **Waddell, L.A.**
Upagupta, the fourth Buddhist patriarch, and high priest of Asoka. *Journal of the Asiatic Society of Bengal*, Vol. 66, pt. 1, No. 1, 1897: 76-84.

JAINA

210. **Agrawala, V.S.**
Jain dharma aur Braj. In Radhey Shyam Dwivedi, ed., *Braj Vaibhav*. Mathura, Bharati Anusandhan Bhawan, 1972: 81-84. (Hindi)

211. _____.
Pracheen Mathura me Jaina dharma ka vaibhav. *Shraman*, Vol. 4, No. 10, August 1953: 7-12. (Hindi)

212. **Chatterjee, Asim Kumar**
A comprehensive history of Jainism. Calcutta, Firma K.L.M. Private Limited, 1978-1984. 2 Vols.

213. **Deo, S.B.**
Expansion of Jainism. In A. Ghosh, ed., *Jaina art and architecture*, Vol. 1. New Delhi, Bharatiya Jnanpith, 1974: 22-34.

214. _____.
Jaina church at Mathura. In Neelkantha Purushottam Joshi, ed., *Jain-nibandh-mala*, Vol. 1. Rampur, Babu Anand Kumar Jain Sansthan, 1977: 91-96.

215. **Dhaky, M.A.**
Urjayatgiri and Jina Aristanemi. *Journal of the Indian Society of Oriental Art*, New Series, Vol. 11, 1980: 1-33.

216. **Folkert, Kendall W.**
Jain religious life at ancient Mathura: The heritage of late victorian interpretation. In Doris Meth Srinivasan, ed., *Mathura: The cultural heritage*. New Delhi, American Institute of Indian Studies, 1989: 103-112.

217. **Jain, Balbhadra**
Bharat ke Digamber jain tirtha. Bombay, Bharatavershiya Digamber Jain Tirth-kshetra Committee, 1978. Vol. 1. (Hindi)

218. **Jain, Jagdish Chandra**
Bharat ke pracheen Jain tirtha. Varanasi, Jain Sanskriti Sanshodhan Mandal, 1952. (Hindi)

219. **Jain, J.P.**
Genesis of Jaina literature and the Saraswata movement. *Bulletin of Museums & Archaeology in U.P.*, No. 9, June 1972: 30-33.

220. **Jain, Jyoti Prasad**
Pracheen Mathura ke Jaino ki sangha-vyavastha. *Anekant*. Vol. 17, No. 5, December 1964: 217-219. (Hindi)

221. _____.
Uttar Pradesh ke Jain tirtha evam sanskritik kendra. In Jyoti Prasad Jain, ed., *Bhagwan Mahavira smriti grantha*. Lucknow, Shri Mahavira Nirvana Samiti, 1975: 29-66. (Hindi)

222. Jainism in Uttar Pradesh. *Jain Journal*, Vol. 3, No. 4, April 1969: 183-189.

223. **Puri, B.N.**
Jainism in Mathura in the early centuries of the Christian era. In *Shri Mahavir Jain Vidyalaya Golden Jubilee Volume*, Vol. 1. Bombay, Shri Mahavira Jaina Vidyalaya, 1968: 156-161.

224. **Shah, Umakant P.** and **Bender, Ernest**
Mathura and Jainism. In Doris Meth Srinivasan, ed., *Mathura: The cultural heritage*. New Delhi, American Institute of Indian Studies, 1989: 209-213.

225. _____.
Mathura and Jainism. *Journal of the Oriental Institute*, Vol. 36, Nos. 1-4, September 1986-June 1987: 87-95.

226. **Upadhyaya, S.C.**
Kusana-kalin Mathura ki Jaina sabhyata. *Shraman*, Vol. 7, No. 2, December 1955: 17-18, 22. (Hindi)

ARCHAEOLOGY

227. **Agrawala, P.K.**
Two relic-caskets from Mathura. *Puratattva*, No. 3, 1969-70: 49-52.

228. **Agrawala, R.C.**
Early Indian bone figures in the National Museum, New Delhi. *East and West,* New Series, Vol. 18, Nos. 3-4, September-December 1968: 311-314.

229. ——.
A newly discovered sherd from Sonkh and the kinnari pot from Begram. *East and West,* New Series. Vol. 26, Nos. 3-4, September-December 1976: 341-342.

230. **Bajpai, K.D.**
Archaeology in Uttar Pradesh. Lucknow, Department of Education, U.P., 1953.

231. **Banerji-Sastri, A.**
Remains of a prehistoric civilisation in the Gangetic valley. In *Commemorative essays presented to Professor Kashinath Bapuji Pathak.* Poona, Bhandarkar Oriental Research Institute, 1934: 248-261.

232. **Brajesh Krishna**
Kuchh etihasik uttakhanana. *Uttar Pradesh,* Vol. 9, No. 12, May 1981: 55-57, 61. (Hindi)

233. **Buhler, G.**
Some notes on past and future archaeological explorations in India. *Journal of the Royal Asiatic Society of Great Britain and Ireland,* 1895: 649-660.

234. **Cunningham, A.**
Archaeological Survey of India, Vol. 1: Four reports made during the year 1862-65: 231-244.

235. _____.
Archaeological Survey of India, Vol. 3: Report for the year 1971-72: 13-46.

236. _____.
Archaeological Survey of India, Vol. 17: Report of a tour in the Central provinces and Lower Gangetic Doab in 1881-82: 107-112.

237. _____.
Archaeological Survey of India, Vol. 20: Report of a tour in eastern Rajputana in 1982-83: 30-54.

238. _____.
Report of the proceedings of the Archaeological Surveyor to the Government of India for the season of 1862-63: Mathura. *Journal of the Asiatic Society of Bengal*, Vol. 34, Pt. 1, No. 3, 1865: 155-167.

239. Excavations at Mathura. *Annual progress report of the Archaeological Survey Circle, North-Western Provinces and Oudh, for the year ending 30th June, 1896*: 1-2.

240. Excavations at Mathura, district Mathura. *Indian Archaeology: A Review*, 1973-74: 31-32.

241. Excavation at Mathura, district Mathura. *Indian Archaeology: A Review*, 1974-75: 48-50.

242. Excavation at Mathura, district Mathura. *Indian Archaeology: A Review*, 1975-76: 53-55.

243. Excavation at Mathura, district Mathura. *Indian Archaeology: A Review*, 1976-77: 54-56.

244. Excavations at Sonkh, district Mathura. *Indian Archaeology: A Review*, 1966-67: 40-43.

245. Excavation at Sonkh, district Mathura. *Indian Archaeology: A Review*, 1968-69: 40.

246. Excavation at Sonkh, district Mathura. *Indian Archaeology: A Review*, 1969-70: 42-43.

247. Excavation at Sonkh, district Mathura. *Indian Archaeology: A Review*, 1970-71: 39-40.

248. Excavation at Sonkh, district Mathura. *Indian Archaeology: A Review*, 1971-72: 47-48.

249. Excavation at Sonkh, district Mathura. *Indian Archaeology: A Review*, 1972-73: 33-35.

250. Exploration. *Annual progress report of the Superintendent, Hindu and Buddhist monuments, Northern Circle for the year ending 31st March 1912*: 2.

251. Exploration. *Annual progress report of the Superintendent, Hindu and Buddhist monuments, Northern Circle for the year ending 31st March 1913*: 4-5.

252. Exploration at Naujheel, district Mathura. *Indian Archaeology: A Review*, 1983-84: 89.

253. Exploration in district Mathura. *Indian Archaeology: A Review*, 1974-75: 48.

254. Exploration in district Mathura. *Indian Archaeology: A Review*, 1982-83: 99.

255. Exploration in district Kanpur, Mathura and Sitapur. *Indian Archaeology: A Review*, 1970-71: 39.

256. Exploration: Muttra. *Annual progress report of the Superintendent, Hindu and Buddhist monuments, Northern Circle for the year ending 31st March 1917*: 7-10.

257. **Fuhrer, A.**
The monumental antiquities and inscriptions, in the North-Western provinces and Oudh. Allahabad, Government Press, 1891.

258. **Fussman, Gerard**
The Mat devakula: A new approach to its understanding. In Doris Meth Srinivasan, ed., *Mathura: The cultural heritage*. New Delhi, American Institute of Indian Studies, 1989: 193-199.

259. **Gaur, R.C.**
Mathura-Govardhana region: An archaeological assessment in historical perspective. In S.K. Maity and Upendra Thakur, ed., *Indological Studies: Professor D.C. Sircar commemoration volume*. New Delhi, Abhinav Publications, 1987: 103-113.

260. **Ghosh, A.**
The Kushan levels at some excavated sites in North India. In *Central Asia in the Kushan period: Proceedings of the International Conference of the History, Archaeology and Culture of Central Asia in the Kushan period. 1968*, Vol. 2. UNESCO, 1975: 108-112.

261. ____.
The Kushan levels at some excavated sites in north India. *Journal of the Ganganatha Jha Kendriya Sanskrit Vidyapeetha*, Vol. 27, pts. 3-4, July-October 1971: 233-242.

262. **Gupta, P.L.**
Uttar Pradesh me tamra yug. *Uttar Pradesh*, Vol. 9, No. 12, May 1981: 3-9. (Hindi)

263. **Hartel, Herbert**
Die Kusana-horizonte im hugel von Sonkh (Mathura). In Herbert Hartel and Volker Moeller, ed., *Indologen-tagung 1971*. Wiesbaden, Franz Steiner Verlag GMBH, 1973: 1-24. (German)

264. ____.
Excavations at Sonkh (Mathura district) 1966-67. *Bulletin of Museums & Archaeology in U.P.*, No. 1, March 1968: 3-8.

265. ____.
Excavations at Sonkh (Mathura district) 1967-68. *Bulletin of Museums & Archaeology in U.P.*, No. 2, December 1968: 3-5.

266. ____.
Excavations at Sonkh (Mathura district) 1968-69. *Bulletin of Museums & Archaeology in U.P.*, No. 3, June 1969: 1-5.

267. ____.
Excavations at Sonkh (Mathura district) 1969-70. *Bulletin of Museums & Archaeology in U.P.*, Nos. 5-6, June & December 1970: 1-4.

268. ____.
New Kusana finds from Sonkh. *Bulletin of Museums & Archaeology in U.P.*, No. 3, June 1969: 71-72.

269. ____.
Pottery of Mathura. In Doris Meth Srinivasan, ed., *Mathura: The cultural heritage*. New Delhi, American Institute of Indian Studies, 1989: 181-192.

270. ____.
Some results of the excavations at Sonkh. In *German Scholars on India*, Vol. 2. Bombay, Nachiketa Publications, 1976: 69-99.

271. ____.
Some results of the excavations at Sonkh: A preliminary report. New Delhi, National Museum, 1977.

272. **Joshi M.C.** and **Sinha, A.K.**
Chronology of Mathura: An assessment. *Puratattva*, No. 10; 1978-79: 39-44.

273. **Joshi, M.C.**
Mathura as an ancient settlement. In Doris Meth Srinivasan, ed., *Mathura: The cultural heritage*. New Delhi, American Institute of Indian Studies, 1989: 165-170.

274. **Joshi, Munish Chandra** and **Sinha, Ashok Kumar**
Puratattivik sakshya aur pracheen Mathura ki khoj. *Uttar Pradesh*, Vol. 9, No. 12, May 1981: 14-19. (Hindi)

275. **Joshi, N.P.** and **Rastogi, S.K.**
Kankali ki purasampada. In Neelkantha Purushottam Joshi, ed., *Jain-nibandh-mala*, Vol.1. Rampur, Babu Anand Kumar Jain Sansthan, 1977: 81-90. (Hindi)

276. **Khanna, Amar Nath**
Archaeology of India: Retrospect and prospect. New Delhi, Clarion Books, 1981.

277. **Lal, B.B.**
Excavation at Hastinapura and other explorations in the Upper Ganga and Sutlej basins 1950-52. *Ancient India*, Nos. 10-11, 1954-1955: 5-151.

278. _____.
Mathura: A re-assessment of the chronology of the crucial northern black polished ware horizons. *Man and Environment*, Vol. 9, 1985: 109-112.

279. **Margabandhu, C.**
Etched beads from Mathura excavations—a note. In Doris Meth Srinivasan, ed., *Mathura: The cultural heritage*. New Delhi, American Institute of Indian Studies, 1989: 200-205.

280. Mathura. *Indian Archaeology: A Review*, 1954-55: 15-16.

281. Muttra. *Annual progress report of the Superintendent, Hindu and Buddhist monuments, Northern Circle for the year ending 31st March 1918:* 11.

282. N.B.P. ware, ring-wells and a Buddha image, Mathura. *Indian Archaeology: A Review*, 1971-72: 80.

283. **Nigam, M.L.**
Glimpses of Jainism through archaeology in Uttar Pradesh. In *Shri Mahavir Jain Vidyalaya Golden Jubilee Volume*, Vol. 1. Bombay, Shri Mahavira Jaina Vidyalaya, 1968: 213-220.

284. **Ojha, K.C.**
Archaeological search for ancient Mathura. *Journal of Indian Museums*, Vol. 29, 1973: 33-39.

285. **Purushottam Singh**
Early historical archaeology of Uttar Pradesh — recent discoveries. *Journal of the Bihar Research Society*, Vols. 65-66, 1979-80: 132-154.

286. Radiocarbon dates: Sonkh, district Mathura. *Indian Archaeology: A Review*, 1969-70: 68.

287. **Roy, T.N.**
The Ganges civilization. New Delhi, Ramanand Vidya Bhawan, 1983.

288. **Shaffer, Jim G.**
Mathura: A protohistoric perspective. In Doris Meth Srinivasan, ed., *Mathura: The cultural heritage*. New Delhi, American Institute of Indian Studies, 1989: 171-180.

289. **Sharma, R.C.**
Antiquarian wealth from Sonkh. In Upendra Thakur and Yugal Kishore Mishra ed., *The heritage of India: L.N. Mishra commemoration volume*. Bodh Gaya, L.N. Mishra Commemoration Volume Publication Committee, 1978: 183-187.

290. **Sharma, R.S.**
Decay of Gangetic towns in Gupta and post-Gupta times. *Journal of Indian History*, Golden Jubilee Volume, 1973: 135-150.

291. **Singh, Ram Chandra**
Hamare sanskritik dharohar: Pracheen smarak. *Uttar pradesh*, Vol. 9, No. 12, May 1981: 46-48. (Hindi)

292. **Smith, R. Morton**
Bead-and-reel in India. *East and West*, New Series, Vol. 25, Nos. 3-4, September-December 1975: 439-454.

293. **Thapar, B.K.**
Digging up the past—some recent archaeological finds. *Times of India Annual*, 1977: 79-86.

294. Thermoluminescence dates: Mathura. *Indian Archaeology: A Review*, 1980-81: 105. (Hindi)

295. **Upadhyaya, Kapiladev**
Vrandavan ke teele evam puratattviya avshesa In Thakur Prasad Verma and others, ed., *Yugayugina Vraja*. Varanasi, Bharatiya Itihasa Samkalana Samiti, U.P., 1988: 33-38. (Hindi)

296. **Venis, A.**
Recent excavations at Muttra. *Journal of the U.P. Historical Society*, Vol. 1, pt. 2, June 1918: 141-143.

297. **Vogel, J. Ph.**
Archaeological exploration in India, 1910-11. *Journal of the Royal Asiatic Society of Great Britain and Ireland*, 1912: 113-132.

298. _____.
Exacavations at Mathura. *Archaeological Survey of India Annual Report*, 1911-12: 120-133.

299. _____.
The sacrificial posts of Isapur. *Archaeological Survey of India Annual Report*, 1910-11: 40-48.

300. **Waddington, Hilary**
Preliminary report on the excavation of a mound at Maholi near Muttra, United Provinces, 1940. *Journal of the U.P. Historical Society*, Vol. 15, pt. 2, December 1942: 135-139.

EPIGRAPHY

301. **Agrawala, P.K.**, ed.
Imperial Gupta epigraphs. Varanasi, Books Asia, 1983.

302. **Agrawala, V.S.**
Further new inscriptions from Mathura. *Journal of the U.P. Historical Society*, Vol. 12, pt. 1, July 1939: 22-31.

303. _____.
Ten inscriptions from Mathura. *Journal of the U.P. Historical Society*, Vol. 10, Pt. 1, July 1937: 1-6.

304. _____.
The use of a Scythian title in a Mathura image inscription. *Journal of the Bihar Research Society*, Vol. 38, pt. 2, June 1952: 230-232.

305. _____.
The use of a Scythian title in a Mathura image inscription. *Journal of the U.P. Historical Society*, Vols. 24-25, 1951-1952: 225-227.

306. Another pillar-base in the Archaeological Museum, Mathura. *Annual Report on Indian Epigraphy*, 1972-73: 117 (c-3645)

307. **Bailey, H.W.**
Kusanica. *Bulletin of the School of Oriental and African Studies*, Vol. 14, pt. 3, 1952: 420-434.

308. **Bajpai, K.D.**
An ayagapatta inscription from Mathura. *Journal of the Epigraphical Society of India*, Vol. 8, 1981: 26-30.

309. _____.
New reading of the inscription on sculpture No. J. 20 in the Provincial Museum, Lucknow. *Proceedings and Transactions of the All-India Oriental Conference*, Session 16, Vol. 2, 1951: 233-235.

310. _____.
Three new Kushana inscriptions from Mathura. *Jaina Antiquary,* Vol. 16, No. 1, June 1950: 13-16.

311. _____.
Two new dated Kushana inscriptions from Mathura. *Indian History Congress Proceedings,* Session 15, 1952: 111-112.

312. _____.
Two new dated Kushana inscriptions from Mathura. *Jaina Antiquarry,* Vol. 18, No. 2, December 1952: 39-40.

313. **Bajpeyi, Kalyani**
Jainism in early inscriptions of Mathura. In D.C. Sircar, ed., *Religion and culture of the Jains.* Calcutta, University of Calcutta, 1973: 36-45.

314. _____.
Official designations in early Mathura inscriptions. In D.C. Sircar, ed., *Early Indian political and administrative systems.* Calcutta, University of Calcutta, 1972: 130-139.

315. _____.
Women in early Mathura epigraphs. In D.C. Sircar, ed., *Social life in ancient India.* Calcutta, University of Calcutta, 1971: 72-75.

316. **Bandyopadhyaya, R.D.**
The discovery of seven new-dated records of the Scythian period. *Journal & Proceedings of the Asiatic Society of Bengal,* New Series, Vol. 5, 1909: 271-277.

317. _____.
Mathura inscriptions in the Indian Museum. *Journal & Proceedings of the Asiatic Society of Bengal,* New Series, Vol. 5, 1909 : 237-244.

318. **Banerjee, Manabandu**
A Study of Important Gupta inscriptions. Calcutta, Sanskrit Pustak Bhandar, 1976.

319. **Banerjee, Priyatosh**
Mathura inscription of Devaputra Kaniska. *Journal of the Bihar Research Society,* Vol. 30, pt. 2, June 1944: 203-204.

320. _____.
The Patna Brahmi inscription from Mathura. *Journal of the Bihar Research Society,* Vol. 30, pt. 2, June 1944: 204-205.

321. **Banerji, Rakhal Das**
New Brahmi inscriptions of the Scythian period. *Epigraphia Indica,* Vol. 10, 1909-10: 106-121.

322. **Banerji, R.D.**
The Scythian period of Indian history. *Indian Antiquary,* Vol. 37, 1908: 25-75.

323. **Barnett, L.D.**
Inscriptions in the Victoria and Albert Museum. *Journal of the Royal Asiatic Society of Great Britain and Ireland,* 1915: 337-339.

324. **Barth, A.**
The inscription P. on the Mathura Lion-Capital. *Indian Antiquary,* Vol. 37, 1908: 245-250.

325. Base of a Bodhisattva image in the Provincial Museum, Lucknow. *Annural Report on Indian Epigraphy,* 1972-73: 114 (c-3621).

326. Base of a headless image of the Buddha kept in the Lucknow Provincial Museum. *Annual Report on Indian Epigraphy,*1977-78: 132 (c-4327).

327. Base of a pillar. *Annual Report on Indian Epigraphy,* 1962-63: 79 (B-252).

328. Base of a pillar. *Annual Report on Indian Epigraphy,* 1975-76: 117 (c-4218).

329. Base of a seated figure of a Jaina Tirthankara in the Provincial Museum, Lucknow. *Annual Report on Indian Epigraphy,* 1972-73: 114 (c-3620).

330. Base of an image from Kankali Tila. *Annual Report on Indian Epigraphy,* 1952-53: 77 (B-524).

331. **Bergny, A.V.**
Notes on some Brahmi-Kharosthi inscriptions on Indian coins. *Journal of the Royal Asiatic Society of Great Britain and Ireland,* 1900: 409-421.

332. Between the feat of a colossal seated figure of a king. *Annual Report on Indian Epigraphy,* 1966-67: 56-57 (c-2438).

333. **Bhandarkar, D.R.**
A Kushana stone-inscription and the question about the origin of the Saka era. *Journal of the Bombay Branch of the Royal Asiatic Society,* Vol. 20, 1897-1900: 269-302.

334. _____.
Mathura pillar inscription of Chandragupta II: G.E. 61. *Epigraphia Indica*, Vol. 21, 1931-32: 1-9.

335. **Bhattacharya, Gouriswar**
On the fragmentary, bi-scriptual pedestal inscription from Mathura. *Indian Museum Bulletin*, Vol. 19, 1984: 27-30.

336. **Bloch, Theodor**
An ancient inscribed Buddhistic statue from Cravasti. *Journal of the Asiatic Society of Bengal*, Vol. 67, pt. 1, No. 4, 1898: 274-290.

337. _____.
Mathura image inscription of the year 33 of Huvishka. *Epigraphia Indica*, Vol. 8, 1905-06: 181-182.

338. Brahmi inscription, Mathura, district Mathura. *Indian Archaeology: A Review*, 1979-80: 91.

339. A brick in the Archaeological Museum, Mathura. *Annural Report on Indian Epigraphy*, 1972-73: 80 (B-386).

340. Brick inscription, Brindaban, district Mathura. *Indian Archaeology: A Review*, 1979-80: 90-91.

341. Bricks in the Archaeological Museum, Mathura, No. 1. *Annual Report on Indian Epigraphy*, 1972-73: 116 (c-3636).

342. Bricks in the Archaeological Museum, Mathura, No. 2. *Annual Report on Indian Epigraphy*, 1972-73: 116 (c-3637).

343. Broken brick. *Annual Report on Indian Epigraphy*, 1959-60: 133 (c-558).

344. Broken pedestal. *Annual Report on Indian Epigraphy*, 1959-60: 131 (c-543).

345. Broken pedestal. *Annual Report on Indian Epigraphy*, 1959-60: 132 (c-551).

346. Broken pedestal of an image of seated Bodhisattva in the provincial Museum, Lucknow. *Annual Report on Indian Epigraphy*, 1972-73: 116 (c-3635).

347. Broken piece of a large slab. *Annual Report on Indian Epigraphy*, 1952-53: 75 (B-493).

348. Broken piece of another ornamental slab from Kankali Tila. *Annual Report on Indian Epigraphy*, 1952-53: 75 (B- 504).

349. Broken sculptured slab. *Annual Report on Indian Epigraphy*, 1959-60: 132 (c-553).

350. Broken slab from Kankali Tila. *Annual Report on Indian Epigraphy*, 1952-53: 75 (B-497).

351. Broken slab in the Archaeological Museum, Mathura. *Annual Report on Indian Epigraphy*, 1972-73: 81 (B-393).

352. Broken slab with an elephant figure. *Annual Report on Indian Epigraphy*, 1959-60: 133 (c-566).

353. Buddha image in a niche. Mathura Museum, Mathura. *Annual Report on Indian Epigraphy*, 1957-58: 72 (B- 598).

354. Buddha image. Provincial Museum, Lucknow. *Annual Report on Indian Epigraphy*, 1959-60: 131 (c-536).

355. A Buddhist image in the Archaeological Museum, Mathura. *Annual Report on Indian Epigraphy*, 1972-73: 117 (c-3646).

356. Buddhist image. Provincial Museum, Lucknow. *Annual Report on Indian Epigraphy*, 1959-60: 131 (c-533).

357. **Buhler, G.**
Dr. Bhagvanlal Indraji interpretation of the Mathura Lion pillar inscriptions. *Journal of the Royal Asiatic Society of Great Britain and Ireland*, 1894: 525-540.

358. _____.
Epigraphic discoveries at Mathura. *Journal of the Royal Asiatic Society of Great Britain and Ireland*, 1896: 578-581.

359. _____.
Further Jaina inscriptions from Mathura. *Epigraphia Indica*, Vol. 1, 1892: 393-397.

360. _____.
Further Jaina inscriptions from Mathura. *Epigraphia Indica*, Vol. 2, 1894: 195-212.

361. _____.
The Mahaban prasasti of Samvat 1207. *Epigraphia Indica*, Vol. 2, 1894: 275-279.

362. _____.
The Mathura prasasti of the reign of Vijayapala. *Epigraphia Indica*, Vol.1, 1892: 287-293.

363. _____.
New Jaina inscriptions from Mathura. *Epigraphia Indica*, Vol. 1, 1892: 371-393.

364. _____.
Specimens of Jaina sculptures from Mathura. *Epigraphia Indica*, Vol. 2, 1894: 311-323.

365. **Chakraborti, Haripada**
India as reflected in the inscriptions of the Gupta period. New Delhi, Munshiram Manoharlal, 1978.

366. **Chakravarti, N.P.**
Epigraphy: Curzon Museum of Archaeology, Muttra. *Archaeological Survey of India Annual Report*, 1935-36: 113-114.

367. **Chakravarti, S.N.**
Development of the Bengali alphabet from the fifth century A.D. to the end of the Muhammadan rule. *Journal of the Royal Asiatic Society of Bengal, Letters*, Vol. 4, 1938: 351-391.

368. **Chakravarti, Shyamal Kanti**
A descriptive catalogue of the Prakrit and Sanskrit inscriptions in the Epigraphy Gallery, Indian Museum. Calcutta, Indian Museum, 1977.

369. **Chattopadhyaya, B.D.**
On a bi-scriptual epigraph of the Kusana period from Mathura. *Journal of Ancient Indian History*, Vol. 13, pts. 1-2, 1980-82: 277-284.

370. **Chattopadhyaya, Kshetresachandra**
Laksam kotim alekhayat. In Bimala Churn Law, ed., *D.R. Bhandarkar Volume*. Calcutta, Indian Research Institute, 1940: 177-180.

371. **Chhabra, Bahadurchand** and **Gai, Govind Swamirao,** ed.
Corpus inscriptionum indicarum, Vol. 3: Inscriptions of the early Gupta kings. New Delhi, Archaeological Survey of India, 1981.

372. **Chhabra, B. Ch.**
Curzon Museum inscription of Kaniskha's reign; year 23. *Epigraphia Indica*, Vol. 28, 1949-50: 42-44.

373. Clay sealing inscriptions, Mathura. *Indian Archaeology: A Review*, 1971-72: 61.

374. **Cunningham, A.**
Note on the preceding Mathura inscpriptions. *Journal of the Royal Asiatic Society of Great Britain and Ireland*, New Series, Vol. 5, 1871: 193-196.

375. **Damsteegt, Theo.**
Epigraphical hybrid Sanskrit. Leiden, E.J. Brill, 1978.

376. _____.
The pre-Kusana and Kusana inscriptions and the supersession of Prakrit by Sanskrit in North India in general and at Mathura in particular. In Doris Meth Srinivasan, ed., *Mathura: The cultural heritage*. New Delhi, American Institute of Indian Studies, 1989: 298-307.

377. **Dani, Ahmad Hasan**
Mathura Lion capital inscription (A palaeographical study). *Journal of the Asiatic Society of Pakistan*, Vol. 5, 1960: 128-147.

378. Dargah 'Idu Shah behind the row of shops in the Bazar, Sadabad. Slab in the north wall. *Annual Report on Indian Epigraphy*, 1972-73: 150 (D-261).

379. **Das, Kalyani**
Early inscriptions of Mathura—a study. Calcutta, Punthi Pustak, 1980.

380. **Deb, Harit Krishna**
Mathura Lion-Capital inscriptions. *Journal of the Royal Asiatic Society of Bengal, Letters*, Vol. 10, No. 1, 1944: 13-37.

381. _____.
St. Thomas and a Kushan king. *Journal and Proceedings of the Asiatic of Bengal*, New Series, Vol. 29, 1933: 311-312.

382. _____.
Scythian tribal names in a Mathura epigraph. *Indian Historical Quarterly*, Vol. 9, No. 3, September 1933: 800-802.

383. **Diskalkar, D.B.**
A new inscription of Chandragupta II of G.S. 61 found in Mathura. *Annals of the Bhandarkar Oriental Research Institute*, Vol. 18, pt. 2, January 1937: 166-170.

384. The dome of a miniature Buddhist stupa in the Archaeological Museum, Mathura. *Annual Report on Indian Epigraphy*, 1972-73: 117 (c-3642).

385. Door-jamb. *Annual Report on Indian Epigraphy*, 1958-59: 115 (c-430).

386. Door-jamb. *Annual Report on Indian Epigraphy*, 1959-60: 132 (c-554).

387. **Dowson, J.,** tr.
Ancient inscriptions from Mathura. *Journal of the Royal Asiatic Society of Great Britain and Ireland,* New Series, Vol. 5, 1871: 182-193.

388. Epitaph, Mathura. *Indian Archaeology: A Review,* 1976-77: 68.

389. Figure of a Yakshi. *Annual Report on Indian Epigraphy,* 1959-60: 132 (c-555).

390. Figure of Kubera. *Annual Report on Indian Epigraphy,* 1959-60: 133 (c-561).

391. Figure of Kubera. Mathura Museum No. 1262. *Annual Report on Indian Epigraphy,* 1959-60: 133(c-562).

392. **Fleet, J.F.**
Corpus inscriptionum indicarum, Vol. 3: Inscriptions of the early Gupta kings and their successors. Varanasi, Indological Book House, 1963.

393. _____.
A hitherto unrecognised Kushan king. *Journal of the Royal Asiatic Society of Great Britain and Ireland,* 1903: 325-334.

394. _____.
The inscription P. on the Mathura Lion-Capital. *Journal of the Royal Asiatic Society of Great Britain and Ireland,* 1905: 154-156.

395. _____.
Moga, Maues and Vonones. *Journal of the Royal Asiatic Society of Great Britain and Ireland,* 1907: 1013-1040.

396. _____.
The name Kushan. *Journal of the Royal Asiatic Society of Great Britain and Ireland,* 1914: 369-381.

397. _____.
Note on a Jain inscription at Mathura. *Journal of the Royal Asiatic Society of Great Britain and Ireland,* 1905: 635-655.

398. _____.
A note on one of the inscriptions on the Mathura Lion-Capital. *Journal of the Royal Asiatic Society of Great Britain and Ireland,* 1904: 703-709.

399. _____.
Vasashka; Vasuskha. *Journal of the Royal Asiatic Society of Great Britain and Ireland,* 1905: 357-358.

400. _____.
Vasiska, the Kusana: Remarks on Dr. Vogel's note. *Journal of the Royal Asiatic Society of Great Britain and Ireland*, 1910: 1315-1317.

401. Four inscriptions, Mathura. *Indian Archaeology: A Reveiw*, 1972-73: 46-47.

402. Fragment of a Buddha image in the courtyard of the Archaeological Museum, Mathura. *Annual Report on India Epigraphy*, 1972-73: 117 (c-3638).

403. Fragment of a pedestal. *Annual Report on Indian Epigraphy*, 1959-60: 133 (c-560).

404. Fragment of a pedestal. *Annual Report on Indian Epigraphy*, 1959-60: 133 (c-568).

405. Fragment of a sculpture in the Archaeological Museum, Mathura. *Annual Report on Indian Epigraphy*, 1972-73: 80 (B-390).

406. Fragment of a stone. Mathura Museum, Mathura. *Annual Report on Indian Epigraphy*, 1955-56: 61 (c-68).

407. Fragment of a stone in the Mathura Museum. *Annual Report on Indian Epigraphy*, 1958-59: 104 (B-788).

408. A fragmentary stone pedestal. Mathura Museum, Mathura. *Annual Report on Indian Epigraphy*, 1956-57: 109 (c-219).

409. A fragmentary stone pedestal. Mathura Museum, Mathura. *Annual Report on Indian Epigraphy*, 1956-57: 109 (c-218).

410. A fragmentary stone pedestal. Mathura Museum, Mathura. *Annual Report on Indian Epigraphy*, 1956-57: 109 (c-220).

411. **Gai, G.S.**
Inscriptions. In A. Ghosh, ed., *Jaina Art and Architecture*, Vol. 3. New Delhi, Bharatiya Jnanpith, 1975: 441-455.

412. _____.
Mathura Jaina inscriptions of the Kusana period—a fresh study. In U.P. Shah and M.A. Dhaky, ed., *Aspects of Jaina Art and Architecture*. Ahmedabad, Gujarat State Committee for the Celebration of 2500th Anniversary of Bhagavan Mahavira Nirvana, 1975: 81-85.

413. _____.
Note on the Mathura pedestal inscription of Kanishka, year 14. *Journal of the Epigraphical Society of India*, Vol. 6, 1979: 12-17.

414. **Ghosal, S.N.**
Mathura Buddha image inscription of the time of Vasudeva. *Visveshvaranand Indological Journal*, Vol. 19, 1981: 188-192.

415. _____.
Mathura image inscription of Vasudeva of the year 80. *Journal of the Asiatic Society*, Vol. 26, 1984: 10-15.

416. _____.
Mathura stone inscription of the time of Sodasa. *Journal of the Asiatic Society*, Vol. 26, 1984: 23-25.

417. Gobind Deo temple, Brindavan. *Annual Report on Indian Epigraphy*, 1958-59: 114 (c-425).

418. Gobind Deo temple. Pillar in north-western inner corner of the mandapa. *Annual Report on Indian Epigraphy*, 1958-59: 115 (c-426).

419. **Goyal, Sriram**
Guptakalina abhilekha. Meerut, Kusumanjali Prakashan, 1984. (Hindi)

420. **Growse, F.S.**
Mathura inscriptions. *Indian Antiquary*, Vol. 6, 1877: 216-219.

421. **Gupta, Sumant**
Guptavanshiya abhilekho ka dharmik adhyayan. New Delhi, Ajay Book Service, 1981. (Hindi)

422. **Gupte, Y.R.**
A Naga figure in the Mathura Museum. *Epigraphia Indica*, Vol. 17, 1923-24: 10-12.

423. **Handa, Devendra**
A Mauryan stupa at Chaneti, Panjab. *Vishveshvaranand Indological Journal*, Vol. 4, pt. 1, March 1966: 75-79.

424. **Hartel, Herbert**
An early coping stone inscription from Mathura. In Gouriswar Bhattacharya, ed., *Deyadharma: Studies in memory of Dr. D.C. Sircar*. Delhi, Sri Satguru Publications, 1986: 101-110.

425. Head of an image. *Annual Report on Indian Epigraphy*, 1959-60: 133 (c-570).

426. Head stone of a grave in the graveyard near the Bus Stand, Sadabad. *Annual Report on Indian Epigraphy*, 1972-73: 150 (D-262).

427. **Hirananda Sastri**
Epigraphy. *Archaeological Survey of India Annual Report*, 1930-1934, pt. 1: 207-208.

428. ——.
Epigraphy: Muttra Museum. *Archaeological Survey of India Annual Report*, 1929-30: 186-187.

429. Horizontal slab in the Archaeological Museum, Mathura. *Annual Report on Indian Epigraphy*, 1972-73: 80 (B-389).

430. An image of a female figure in the Archaeological Museum, Mathura. *Annual Report on Indian Epigraphy*, 1972-73: 80 (B-384).

431. Image of Bodhisattva. Mathura Museum, Mathura. *Annual Report on Indian Epigraphy*, 1957-58: 72 (B-599).

432. Image of Maitreya. *Annual Report on Indian Epigraphy*, 1959-60: 133 (c-563).

433. Inscribed image of Sambhavanatha in the Provincial Museum, Lucknow. *Annual Report on Indian Epigraphy*, 1972-73: 113 (c-3616).

434. Inscriped lamp of clay in the possession of a bullion dealer. *Annual Report on Indian Epigraphy*, 1960-61: 114 (B-622).

435. Inscription on Buddha-image, Mathura. *Indian Archaeology: A Review*, 1976-77: 63-64.

436. Inscription of Huvishka, Kankali Tila, Mathura. *Indian Archaeology : A Review*, 1976-77 : 63.

437. A Jaina image in the Provincial Museum, Lucknow. *Annual Report on Indian Epigraphy*, 1972-73: 114 (c-3618).

438. A Jaina image in the Archaeological Museum, Mathura. *Annual Report on Indian Epigraphy*, 1972-73: 117 (c-3643)

439. Jaina-shilalekh sangraha, Vol. 2-3. Bombay, Sri Manikchandra-Digambar Jain Granthamala, 1952-1957. Vol. 4. Varanasi, Bharatiya Jnanpith, 1961. (Hindi)

440. Jami-mosque. Slab above the main gate. *Annual Report on Indian Epigraphy*, 1975-76: 177 (D-248).

441. Jami mosque. To the left of the main gate. *Annual Report on Indian Epigraphy*, 1975-76: 177 (D- 249).

442. **Janert, Klaus L.**
A Mathura inscription on a Varaha image. *Journal of the Royal Asiatic Society of Great Britain and Ireland,* parts 1-2, 1966: 7-8.

443. **Jayaswal, K.P.**
Another Saisunaka statue (cir 515 B.C.) *Journal of the Bihar and Orissa Research Society,* Vol. 5, pt. 4, December 1919: 550-51.

444. _____.
Chastana's statue and date of Kanishka. *Journal of the Bihar and Orissa Research Society,* Vol. 5, pt. 4, December 1919: 511.

445. _____.
Girdharpur pillar inscription. *Journal of the Bihar and Orissa Research Society,* Vol. 18, pt. 1, 1932: 4-6.

446. _____.
Hathigumpha inscription of the emperor Kharavela. *Journal of the Bihar and Orissa Research Society,* Vol. 13, pts. 3-4, September-December 1927: 221-246.

447. _____.
The statue of Ajatasatru Kunika and a discussion on the origin of Brahmi. *Journal of the Bihar and Orissa Research Society,* Vol. 6, pt. 2, June 1920: 173-204.

448. **Konow, Sten**
Mathura Brahmi inscription of the year 28. *Epigraphia Indica,* Vol. 21, 1931-32: 55-61.

449. _____.
Note on the eras in Indian inscriptions. In *India Antiqua: A volume of oriental studies presented by his friends and pupils to Jean Philippe Vogel.* Leiden, E.J. Brill, 1947: 193-197.

450. _____.
A note on the Girdharpur Brahmi inscription of the year 28. *Indian Historical Quarterly,* Vol. 9, No. 1, March 1933: 145-148.

451. _____.
Note on the Mathura inscription of Samvat 299. In *Commemorative essays presented to Professor Kashinath Bapuji Pathak.* Poona, Bhandarkar Oriental Research Institute, 1934: 262-268.

452. _____.
Rawal spurious inscription of the year 40. *Epigrahia Indica*, Vol. 19, 1927-28: 206-209.

453. Kushana inscription, Govindnagar, district Mathura. *Indian Archaeology: A Review*, 1979-80: 91.

454. Large bowl. *Annual Report on Indian Epigraphy*, 1959-60: 132 (c-556).

455. Large slab. *Annual Report on Indian Epigraphy*, 1958-59: 115 (c-428).

456. Life-size stone statue. *Annual Report on Indian Epigraphy*, 1959-60: 132 (c-552).

457. **Lokesh Chandra**
Stone inscription of Kuluta from Mathura. In *Central Asia in the Kushan period: Proceedings of the International Conference on the History, Archaeology and Culture of Central Asia in the Kushan period, 1968*, Vol. 1. UNESCO, 1974: 334-338.

458. Lower portion of a statue of Buddha. *Annual Report on Indian Epigraphy*, 1959-60: 133 (c-564).

459. **Luders, H.**
Epigraphical notes. *Indian Antiquary*, Vol. 33, 1904: 33-41, 101-109, 149-156.

460. _____.
The era of the Maharaja and the Maharaja Rajatiraja. In Bimala Churn Law, ed., *D.R. Bhandarkar Volume*. Calcutta, Indian Research Institute, 1940: 281-289.

461. _____.
The lingul la in the northern Brahmi script. *Journal of the Royal Asiatic Society of Great Britain and Ireland*, 1911: 1081-1089.

462. _____.
A list of Brahmi inscriptions from the earliest times to about A.D. 400 with the exception of those of Asoka. *Epigraphia Indica*, Appendix, Vol. 10, 1909-10: 1-25.

463. _____.
Mathura inscriptions. Edited by Klaus L. Janert. Gottingen, Vandenhoeck & Ruprecht, 1961.

464. _____.
Mathura stone inscription, dated Samvat 74. *Epigraphia Indica,* Vol. 9, 1907-08: 241-246.

465. _____.
Mathura stone inscription of the time of Sodasa. *Epigraphia Indica,* Vol. 9, 1907-08: 246-248.

466. _____.
On some Brahmi inscriptions in the Lucknow Provincial Museum. *Journal of the Royal Asiatic Society of Great Britain and Ireland,* 1912: 153-179.

467. _____.
Seven Brahmi inscriptions from Mathura and its vicinity. *Epigraphia Indica,* Vol. 24, 1937-38: 194-210.

468. **Majumdar, N.G.**
A new Brahmi inscription from Mathura. *Indian Historical Quarterly,* Vol. 2, No. 3, September 1926: 441-446.

469. **Mehendele, M.A.**
Language of Mathura inscriptions. In Doris Meth Srinivasan, ed., *Mathura: The cultural heritage.* New Delhi, American Institute of Indian Studies, 1989: 247-254.

470. **Mirashi, V.V.**
Date of Mathura pedestal inscription of Kanishka. *Epigraphia Indica,* Vol. 26, 1941-42: 293-297.

471. _____.
Studies in Indology. Nagpur, Vidarbha Samshodhana Mandal, 1960. Vol. 1.

472. Miscellaneous inscriptions, districts Agra, Aligarh, Mathura and Moradabad. *Indian Archaeology: A Review,* 1972-73: 51-52.

473. Miscellaneous inscriptions, Mahaban, district Mathura. *Indian Archaeology: A Review,* 1983-84: 161.

474. **Mitra, Rajendralala**
Notes on Sanskrit inscriptions from Mathura. *Journal of the Asiatic Society of Bengal,* Vol. 39, pt.1, No. 2, 1870: 117-130.

475. Mughal inscription, Mahaban, district Mathura. *Indian Archaeology: A Review,* 1983-84: 161.

476. **Mukherjee, B.N.**
A Mathura inscription of the year 26 and of the period of Huvishka. *Journal of Ancient Indian History,* Vol. 11, 1977-78: 82-84.

477. _____.
A note on a bi-scriptural epigraph of the Kushana period from Mathura. *Journal of Ancient Indian History,* Vol. 13, pts. 1-2, 1980-82: 285-286.

478. **N.R.**
The Mathura pillar inscription of Chandragupta II, G.E. 61. *Indian Antiquary,* Vol. 61, 1932: 117-118.

479. **Nagar, M.M.**
A Buddha image inscription from Mathura. *Indian History Congress, Proceedings,* Session 5, 1941: 163-164.

480. **Nahar, Puran Chand,** comp.
Jaina inscriptions. Calcutta, The Compilor, 1927. Part 2.

481. **Narain, Awadh Kisore** and **Shukla, Mani Shankar,** ed.
Pracheen Bharatiya abhilekh-sangraha. Varanasi, Banaras Hindu Univesity, (n.d.) Vol. 2. (Hindi)

482. Ninth slab in the Indian Museum, Calcutta. *Annual Report on Indian Epigraphy,* 1962-63: 79 (B-248).

483. **Oldenberg, H.**
On the dates of ancient Indian inscriptions and coins. *Indian Antiquary,* Vol. 10, 1881: 213-227.

484. On a grave near the tomb of Ras Khan, Gokul. *Annual Report on Indian Epigraphy,* 1975-76: 176 (D-247).

485. **Pandey, Raj Bali**
Historical and literary inscriptions. Varanasi, Chowkhamba Sanskrit Series Office, 1962.

486. Part of a round ball. *Annual Report on Indian Epigraphy,* 1959-60: 133 (c-571).

487. Pedestal. *Annual Report on Indian Epigraphy,* 1959-60: 132 (c-547).

488. Pedestal. *Annual Report on Indian Epigraphy,* 1959-60: 132 (c-549).

489. Pedestal inscription, Mathura. *Indian Archaeology: A Review,* 1976-77: 64.

490. Pedestal of a Bodhisattva image. *Annual Report on Indian Epigraphy,* 1958-59: 115 (c-431).

491. Pedestal of a broken image. *Annual Report on Indian Epigraphy*, 1959-60: 133 (c-569).

492. Pedestal of a broken image. Mathura Museum, Mathura. *Annual Report on Indian Epigraphy,* 1957-58: 71 (B-591).

493. Pedestal of a broken image. Mathura Museum, Mathura. *Annual Report on Indian Epigraphy*, 1957-58: 71 (B-592).

494. Pedestal of a broken image. Mathura Museum, Mathura. *Annual Report on Indian Epigraphy*, 1957-58: 71 (B-594).

495. Pedestal of a broken image. Mathura Museum, Mathura. *Annual Report on Indian Epigraphy*, 1957-58: 71 (B-597).

496. Pedestal of a broken image from Kankali Tila. *Annual Report on Indian Epigraphy*, 1952-53: 76 (B-512).

497. Pedestal of a broken image of Buddha. Mathura Museum, Mathura. *Annual Report on Indian Epigraphy*, 1957-58: 71 (B-590).

498. Pedestal of a broken sand-stone image of Buddha. *Annual Report on Indian Epigraphy*, 1965-66: 112 (B-677).

499. Pedestal of a broken stone image of standing Buddha. *Annual Report on Indian Epigraphy*, 1965-66: 112 (B-676).

500. Pedestal of a broken Tirthankara image. Mathura Museum, Mathura. *Annual Report on Indian Epigraphy*, 1957-58: 71 (B-593).

501. Pedestal of a Buddha image. *Annual Report on Indian Epigraphy*, 1954-55: 73 (B-525).

502. Pedestal of a Buddha image. Mathura Museum, Mathura. *Annual Report on Indian Epigraphy*,1957-58: 71 (B-595).

503. Pedestal of a Buddha image. Provincial Museum, Lucknow. *Annual Report on Indian Epigraphy*, 1959-60: 131 (c-537).

504. Pedestal of a Jaina image in the Provincial Museum, Lucknow. *Annual Report on Indian Epigraphy*, 1972-73: 114 (c-3619).

505. Pedestal of a Jaina image. Provincial Museum, Lucknow. *Annual Report on Indian Epigraphy,* 1959-60: 131 (c-532).

506. Pedestal of a mutilated image from Kankali Tila. *Annual Report on Indian Epigraphy*, 1952-53: 76 (B-510).

507. Pedestal of a standing female figure. *Annual Report on Indian Epigraphy*, 1958-59: 115 (c-429).

508. Pedestal of a standing male figure. *Annual Report on Indian Epigraphy*, 1958-59: 115 (c-427).

509. Pedestal of a seated Jaina image in the Provincial Museum, Lucknow. *Annual Report on Indian Epigraphy*, 1972-73: 115 (c-3625).

510. Pedestal of a third Jaina image. *Annual Report on Indian Epigraphy*, 1969-70: 75 (c-3001).

511. Pedestal of an image. *Annual Report on Indian Epigraphy*, 1959-60: 133 (c-559).

512. Pedestal of an image in the Archaeological Museum, Mathura. *Annual Report on Indian Epigraphy*, 1972-73: 80 (B-387).

513. Pedestal of an image, No. 1. Mathura Museum, Mathura. *Annual Report on Indian Epigraphy*, 1955-56: 61 (c-60).

514. Pedestal of an image, No. 2. Mathura Museum, Mathura. *Annual Report on Indian Epigraphy*, 1955-56: 61 (c-61).

515. Pedestal of an image, No.3. Mathura, Museum, Mathura. *Annual Report on Indian Epigraphy*, 1955-56: 61 (c-62).

516. Pedestal of an image, No. 4. Mathura, Museum, Mathura. *Annual Report on Indian Epigraphy*, 1955-56: 61 (c-63).

517. Pedestal of an image, No. 5. Mathura, Museum, Mathura.*Annual Report on Indian Epigraphy*, 1955-56: 61 (c-64).

518. Pedestal of an image, No. 6. Mathura, Museum, Mathura. *Annual Report on Indian Epigraphy*, 1955-56: 61 (c-65).

519. Pedestal of an image, No. 7. Mathura, Museum, Mathura. *Annual Report on Indian Epigraphy*, 1955-56: 61 (c-66).

520. Pedestal of an image of a seated Bodhisattva broken vertically into two pieces in the Museum. *Annual Report on Indian Epigraphy*, 1975-76: 117 (c-4216).

521. Pedestal of an image of Vardhamana, seated in meditation, in the Provincial Museum, Lucknow. *Annual Report on Indian Epigraphy*, 1972-73: 115 (c-3623).

522. Pedestal of an image of Amitabha Buddha. *Annual Report on Indian Epigraphy*, 1977-78: 120 (B-301).

523. A pillar-base, cut on the base of the square basement in the Archaeological Museum, Mathura. *Annual Report on Indian Epigraphy*, 1972-73: 117 (c- 3639).

524. A pillar-base in the Archaeological Museum, Mathura. *Annual Report on Indian Epigraphy*, 1972-73: 117 (c-3640).

525. A pillar-base in the Archaeological Museum, Mathura. *Annual Report on Indian Epigraphy*, 1972-73: 117 (c-3641).

526. A pillar-base in the Archaeological Museum, Mathura. *Annual Report on Indian Epigraphy*, 1972-73: 117 (c-3644).

527. A pillar-base in the Mathura Museum. *Annual Report on Indian Epigraphy*, 1971-72: 72 (c-3266).

528. Pillar in the Archaeological Museum, Mathura. *Annual Report on Indian Epigraphy*, 1972-73: 81 (B-392).

529. Pillar in the mandapa of the Govinda Deo temple, Brindavan. *Annual Report on Indian Epigraphy*, 1959-60: 131 (c-542).

530. Pillar-inscription of Kanishka, Mathura. *Indian Archaeology: A Review*, 1976-77: 63.

531. Pillar of the kitchen, Madan Mohan temple, Brindavan. *Annual Report on Indian Epigraphy*, 1959-60: 131 (c-541).

532. Plate in the Archaeological Museum, Mathura. *Annual Report on Indian Epigraphy*, 1960-61: 51 (A-109).

533. Plate in the Archaeological Museum, Mathura, No. 4842. *Annual Report on Indian Epigraphy*, 1960-61: 51 (A-110).

534. Prakrit and Sanskrit inscriptions, Mathura. *Indian Archaeology: A Review*, 1958-59: 63-64.

535. **Puri, B.N.**
The Kusanaputras. *Indian Culture*, Vol. 8, Nos. 2-3, October 1941-March 1942: 191-196.

536. _____.
Mathura Brahmi inscription of the year 84 and its bearing on the later Kusana history. *Indian History Congress, Proceedings*, Session 6, 1943: 77-82.

537. A railing pillar in the Archaeological Museum, Mathura. *Annual Report on Indian Epigraphy*, 1972-73: 117 (c-3647).

538. Raised rim over the front relief of a fragmentary Jina. *Annual Report on Indian Epigraphy*, 1975-76: 117 (c-4217).

539. **Ramachandran, T.N.**
An inscribed Bodhisattva image from Mathura. *Ancient India*, No. 6, 1950: 100-102.

540. **Rastogi, Shailendra Kumar**
Uttar Pradesh ke utkirana Jain lekh aur unka mahattva. In Jyoti Prasad Jain, ed., *Bhagwan Mahavira Smriti grantha.* Lucknow, Shri Mahavira Nirvana Samiti, 1975: 112-116. (Hindi).

541. Red sandstone octagonal pillar in the Archaeological Museum, Mathura. *Annual Report on Indian Epigraphy*, 1972-73: 81 (B-396).

542. Red sandstone pedestal. Indian Museum, Calcutta. *Annual Report on Indian Epigraphy*, 1959-60: 123 (c-433).

543. **Sadhu Ram**
The Mathura pillar inscription of Chandragupta II. Gupta year 61. *Kurukshetra University Research Journal* (Arts and Humanities), Vol. 2, 1968: 13-19.

544. ____.
Three Sarnath inscriptions of the third year of Kaniska—a study. *Vishveshvaranand Indological Journal,* Vol. 2, pt. 2, September 1964: 323-333.

545. **Sahni, Daya Ram**
A Buddhist image inscription from Sravasti. *Archaeological Survey of India Annual Report*, 1908-09: 133-138.

546. ____.
Mathura pedestal inscription of the Kushana year 14. *Epigraphia Indica,* Vol. 19, 1927-28: 96-97.

547. ____.
Seven inscriptions from Mathura. *Epigraphia Indica*, Vol. 19, 1927-28: 65-69.

548. ____.
Three Mathura inscriptions and their bearing on the Kushana dynasty. *Journal of the Royal Asiatic Society of Great Britain and Ireland,* 1924: 399-406.

549. **Satyarthi, H.C.**
Significance of an undated post-Maurya inscription of Mathura bearing on slavery. *Indian History Congress, Proceedings,* Session 38, 1977: 779-783.

550. Sculpture representing seated Siva and Parvati figures. *Annual Report on Indian Epigraphy,* 1559-60: 133 (c-572).

551. Sculptured slab. *Annual Report on Indian Epigraphy*, 1959-60: 133 (c-573).

552. Sculptured stone. *Annual Report on Indian Epigraphy*, 1959-60: 133 (c-567).

553. Sculptured stone slab in the Provincial Museum, Lucknow. *Annual Report on Indian Epigraphy*, 1972-73: 114 (c-3617).

554. Sealing, Mathura. *Indian Archaeology: A Review*, 1967-68: 56.

555. Seals deposited in the Archaeological Museum, Mathura, Seal Nos. 1-20. *Annual Report on Indian Epigraphy*, 1963-64: 177-179. (c-131-150).

556. Seated Buddha image in the Archaeological Museum, Mathura. *Annual Report on Indian Epigraphy*, 1972-73: 80 (B-388).

557. Seated image. *Annual Report on Indian Epigraphy*, 1959-60: 132 (c-557).

558. **Shah, U.P.**
The Jaina inscriptions from Mathura. In Ramesh Chandra Gupta, ed., *Aastha aur Chintana: Acharyaratna Shri Desh Bhushanji Maharaj abhinandan granth*. Delhi, Acharyaratna Shri Desh Bhsushanji Maharaj Abhinandan Granth Samiti, 1987: 17-18.

559. **Sharma, R.C.**
New inscription from Mathura. *Bulletin of Museums & Archaeology in U.P.*, No. 8, December 1971: 24-28.

560. _____.
New inscriptions from Mathura. In Doris Meth Srinivasan, ed., *Mathura: The cultural heritage*. New Delhi, American Institute of Indian Studies, 1989: 308-315.

561. _____.
A new inscription from Mathura. *Journal of the Oriental Institute*, Vol. 21, Nos. 1-2, September-December 1971: 103-106.

562. _____.
New inscription of Sodasa from Mathura. *Epigraphia Indica*, Vol. 40, pt. 5, April 1974: 171-174.

563. ____.
Newly discovered inscription of the reign of Mahakshatrapa Sodasa from Mathura. In Vijaya Shankar Srivastava, ed., *Cultural Contours of India: Dr. Satya Prakash Felicitation Volume*. New Delhi, Abhinav Publications, 1981: 94-100.

564. **Sharma, Tej Ram**
Personal and geographical names in the Gupta inscriptions. Delhi, Concept Publishing Company, 1978.

565. **Shastri, Ajay Mitra**
Modification of early Brahmi into middle Brahmi and late Brahmi stages at Mathura. In Doris Meth Srinivasan, ed. *Mathura: The cultural heritage*. New Delhi, American Institute of Indian Studies, 1989: 316-321.

566. **Sircar, D.C.**
A Brahmi inscription from Mathura. *Bharatiya Vidya*, Vol. 14, 1953: 6-9.

567. ____.
Brahmi inscriptions from Mathura. *Epigraphia Indica*, Vol. 34, 1961-62: 9-13.

568. ____.
A Brahmi Jaina inscription from Mathura. In Vijaya Shankar Srivastava, ed., *Cultural Contours of India: Dr. Satya Prakash Felicitation Volume*. New Delhi, Abhinav Publications, 1981: 92-93.

569. ____.
Date of Mankuwar Buddha image inscription of the time of Kumaragupta I. *Journal of Ancient Indian History*, Vol. 3, 1969-70: 133-137.

570. ____.
An early inscribed image of Indra. *Indian Museum Bulletin*, Vol. 16, 1981: 7-9.

571. ____.
A fragmentary inscription from Mathura. *Journal of the U.P. Historical Society*, New Series, Vol. 2, pt. 2, 1954: 10-14.

572. ____.
Fragmentary Maurya inscription from Mathura. *Epigraphia Indica*, Vol. 32, 1957-58: 207-212.

573. _____.
Garga-Yavana and Kala-Yavana. *Journal of Ancient Indian History,* Vol. 3, 1969-70: 141-144.

574. _____.
Indian epigraphy. Delhi, Motilal Banarsidass, 1965.

575. _____.
Kuluta inscription from Mathura. *Indian Museum Bulletin,* Vol. 7, No. 1, January 1972: 14-15.

576. _____.
Mathura image inscription of Vasudeva. *Epigraphia Indica,* Vol. 30, 1953-54: 181-184.

577. _____.
Note on inscription of Nripamitra. *Epigraphia Indica,* Vol. 35, 1963-64: 200.

578. _____.
A note on the Mathura inscription of Chandragupta II. *Indian Historical Quarterly,* Vol. 18, No. 3, September 1942: 271-275.

579. _____.
Observations on the study of some epigraphic records from Mathura. In Doris Meth Srinivasan, ed., *Mathura: The cultural heritage.* New Delhi, American Institute of Indian Studies, 1989: 257-260.

580. _____.
Palaeographical and epigraphical evidence on Kaniska's date. In A.L. Basham, ed., *Papers on the date of Kaniska.* Leiden, E.J. Brill, 1968: 278-292.

581. _____.
Select inscriptions bearing on Indian history and civilization. Calcutta, University of Calcutta, 1965. Vol. 1.

582. _____.
Two Brahmi inscriptions. *Journal of the Bihar Research Society,* Vol. 39, pts 1-2, March-June 1953: 41-48.

583. Slab. *Annual Report on Indian Epigraphy,* 1959-60: 132 (c-550).

584. Slab. *Annual Report on Indian Epigraphy,* 1959-60: 133 (c-565).

585. Slab in the Madan Mohan temple, Brindavan. *Annual Report on Indian Epigraphy*, 1959-60: 131 (c-539).

586. Slab in the Madan Mohan temple, Brindavan. *Annual Report on Indian Epigraphy*,1959-60: 131 (c-540).

587. Slab in the Mathura Museum, Mathura. *Annual Report on Indian Epigraphy*, 1956-57: 91 (B-530-A).

588. Slab in the Museum, originally from the tank at Kosi. *Annual Report on Indian Epigraphy*, 1952-53: 97 (c-151).

589. Slab. Provincial Museum, Lucknow. *Annual Report on Indian Epigraphy*, 1959-60: 131 (c-538).

590. A slab showing Varaha representation in the Archaeological Museum, Mathura. *Annual Report on Indian Epigraphy*, 1972-73: 81 (B-391).

591. Slabs in the Patna Museum, No. 2. *Annual Report on Indian Epigraphy*, 1963-64: 59 (B-86).

592. **Smith, Vincent A.**
Kusana inscriptions. *Journal of the Asiatic Society of Great Britain and Ireland*, 1905: 151-152.

593. **Srinivasan, P.R.**
Mathura pillar inscription of the Gupta year 61. *Journal of Ancient Indian History*, Vol. 3, pts. 1-2, 1969-70: 113-122.

594. _____.
Two Brahmi inscriptions from Mathura. *Epigraphia Indica*, Vol. 39, pt. 1, January 1971: 9-12.

595. **Srivastava, V.N.**
Buddha pedestal inscription of Kumara Gupta (G.E. 125). *Bulletin of Museums & Archaeology in U.P.*, No. 1, March 1968: 15-17.

596. **Srivastava, V.N.** and **Joshi, Maheshwar P.**
The Mathura inscription of Yavana era 116. *Bulletin of Museums and Archaeology in U.P.*, Nos. 41-42, June-December 1988: 103-106.

597. **Srivastava, V.N.**
New Kushana inscriptions from Mathura. *Journal of the U.P. Historical Society*, Vol. 7, pt. 1, New Series, 1959: 1-3.

598. _____.
Two image inscriptions from Mathura. *Epigraphia Indica*, Vol. 37, 1967-68: 151-154.

599. Statue of a royal personage. *Annual Report on Indian Epigraphy*, 1959-60: 132 (c-546).

600. **Stein, O.**
Formal elements in Indian inscriptions. *Indian Historical Quarterly*, Vol. 9, No. 1, March 1933: 215-226.

601. Stone bowl on the head. Mathura Museum, Mathura. *Annual Report on Indian Epigraphy*, 1955-56: 61(c-67).

602. Stone head of Bodhisattva. Mathura Museum, Mathura. *Annual Report on Indian Epigraphy*, 1957-58: 71(B-596).

603. Stone in the Archaeological Museum, Mathura. *Annual Report on Indian Epigraphy*, 1960-61: 114 (B-620).

604. Stone in the Archaeological Museum, Mathura. *Annual Report on Indian Epigraphy*; 1972-73: 81 (B-394).

605. Stone in possession of Sri-Krishna-Janma-Bhumi Trust. *Annual Report on Indian Epigraphy*, 1960-61: 114 (B-621).

606. Stone mortar lying with a person. *Annual Report on Indian Epigraphy*, 1959-60: 131 (c-544).

607. Stone mortar lying with a person. *Annual Report on Indian Epigraphy*, 1959-60: 132 (c-545).

608. **Subramonia Iyer, S.**
Mathura inscription of Huvishka, year 50. *Journal of the Epigraphical Society of India*, Vol. 10, 1983: 71-72.

609. _____.
Mathura pedestal inscription, year 46. *Epigraphia Indica*, Vol. 40, pt. 4, January 1974: 168-169.

610. _____.
Two Brahmi inscriptions from Mathura. *Epigraphia Indica*, Vol. 40, pt. 1, April 1973: 19-22.

611. Tablet of homage. *Annual Report on Indian Epigraphy*, 1969-70: 76 (c-3006).

612. Talab-ki-Masjid, Kosi. Loose slab. *Annual Report on Indian Epigraphy*, 1972-73: 149 (D-260).

613. **Tewari, S.P.**
Contributions of Sanskrit inscriptions to lexicography. Delhi, Agam Kala Prakashan, 1987.

614. _____.
Inscription of Suryamitra in the National Museum. *Epigraphia Indica*, Vol. 40, pt. 4, January 1974: 165-167.

615. _____.
Two Kushana inscriptions from Govindnagar. *Epigraphia Indica*, Vol. 40, pt. 5, April 1974: 197-200.

616. **Thakural, Pushpa and Mishra, Pyare Lal**
Mathura Sangrahalaya ka navprapta abhilekh. *Bulletin of Museums and Archaeology in U.P.*, Nos. 41-42, June-December 1988: 109-113. (Hindi)

617. **Thaplyal, K.K.** and **Sharma, R.C.**
Mathura Buddhist image inscription of Jiva, dated years 121 and 15. *Bulletin of Museums and Archaeology in U.P.*, Nos. 29-30, June-December 1982: 17-24.

618. _____.
Mathura Buddhist image inscriptions of Mihiranga. *Bulletin of Museums and Archaeology in U.P.*, No. 25, June 1980: 63-67.

619. _____.
Mathura Buddhist image inscription of Sanghavarman. *Bulletin of Museums and Archaeology in U.P.*, Nos. 35-36, June-December 1985: 1-5.

620. **Thaplyal, Kiran Kumar** and **Srivastava, Arvind**
Mathura stone pedestal inscription of the time of Budhagupta, Gupta year 161. *Journal of the Epigraphical Society of India*, Vol. 9, 1982: 6-11.

621. **Thomas, E.**
Bactrian coins and Indian dates. *Journal of the Royal Asiatic Society of Great Britain and Ireland*, New Series, Vol. 9, 1877: 1-21.

622. **Thomas, F.W.**
The inscriptions of the Mathura Lion-capital. *Epigraphia Indica*, Vol. 9, 1907-08: 135-147.

623. _____.
'Kaniska year 14.' In *India Antiqua: A volume presented by his friends and pupils to Jean Philippe Vogel*. Leiden, E.J. Brill, 1947: 296-303.

624. Two Buddhist image-inscriptions, Mathura. *Indian Archaeology: A Review*, 1965-66: 68.

625. **Upadhyaya, Vasudeva**
Gupta abhilekha. Patna, Bihar Hindi Grantha Akademi, 1974. (Hindi)

626. **Verma, T.P.**
The line of Dhanbhuti. *Journal of the Numismatic Society of India*, Vol. 31, pt. 2, 1969: 143-150.

627. _____.
The palaeography of Brahmi script in North India (from c. 236 B.C. to c. 200 A.D.). Varanasi, Siddharth Prakashan, 1971.

628. _____.
Progress of modification of the alphabet as revealed by coins, seals and inscriptions from Mathura. In Doris Meth Srinivasan, ed., *Mathura: The cultural heritage*. New Delhi, America Institute of Indian Studies, 1989: 261-297.

629. _____.
Uttar Pradesh ke abhilekh. *Uttar Pradesh*, Vol. 9, No. 12, May 1981: 36-40. (Hindi)

630. **Vogel, J.Ph.**
Inscriptions of the third year of Kanishka. *Epigraphia Indica*, Vol. 8, 1905-06: 173-179.

631. _____.
The Kushan king Vasishka. *Journal of the Panjab Historical Society*, Vol. 1, No. 2, 1912: 173-174.

632. _____.
Vasiska, the Kusana. *Journal of the Royal Asiatic Society of Great Britain and Ireland*, 1910: 1311-1314.

633. The waist band of a female figure in red sandstone in the Provincial Museum, Lucknow. *Annual Report on Indian Epigraphy*, 1972-73: 114 (c-3622).

634. A Yaksha figure in the Archaeological Museum, Mathura. *Annual Report on Indian Epigraphy*, 1972-73: 80 (B-385).

635. Yupa. *Annual Report on Indian Epigraphy*, 1959-60: 132 (c-548).

NUMISMATICS

636. **Alteker, A.S.**
New kings and interesting coin types from Kausambi. *Journal of the Numismatic Society of India*, Vol. 4, No. 1, June 1942: 1-6.

637. _____.
Some alleged Naga and Vakataka coins. *Journal of the Numismatic Society of India*, Vol. 5, 1943: 111-134.

638. _____.
Two coins from Mathura. *Journal of the Numismatic Society of India*, Vol. 6, 1944: 24-26.

639. **Bajpai, K.D.**
Braj-mandal me upalabdh Naga, Gupta tatha purvamadhya kaleen sikke. *The Researcher*, Vols. 12-13, 1972-73: 25-28 (Hindi).

640. _____.
A coin of Satyamitra—a new ruler of Mathura. *Journal of the Numismatic Society of India*, Vol. 28, pt. 1, 1966: 42.

641. _____.
Fire-altar (?) on the silver and copper coins of the Guptas. *Bulletin of Ancient Indian History and Archaeology*, No. 1, 1967: 71-72.

642. _____.
Indian numismatic studies. New Delhi, Abhinav Publications, 1976.

643. _____.
The joint issues of the Kshatrapas Hagana and Hagamasha. *Journal of the Numismatic Society of India*, Vol. 25, 1963: 102-103.

644. _____.
The Mitra rulers of Mathura. *Journal of the Numismatic Society of India*, Vol. 42, pts. 1-2, 1980: 1-5.

645. **Banerjea, J.N.**
Two new varieties of old Indian coins. *Indian Historical Quarterly*, Vol. 10, No. 4, December 1934: 723-727.

646. **Brown, C.J.**
The Coins of India. Varanasi, Indological Book House, 1973.

647. **Burn, Richard**
Note on Indian coins and inscriptions. *Journal of the Royal Asiatic Society of Great Britain and Ireland*, 1900: 552-554.

648. **Chakrabortty, Surendra Kisor**
A study of ancient Indian numismatics from the earliest times to the rise of imperial Guptas. Varanasi, Bharatiya Publishing House, 1973.

649. **Chatterjee, C.D.**
Some unique gold and brass coins of the imperial Guptas. *Bulletin of the U.P. Historical Society*, No. 2, 1957: 1-74.

650. **Chattopadhyay, Bhaskar**
The age of the Kushanas—a numismatic study. Calcutta, Punthi Pustak, 1967.

651. _____.
Coins and icons: A study of myths and symbols in Indian numismatic art. Calcutta, Punthi Pustak, 1977.

652. Coins, Govindnagar, district Mathura. *Indian Archaeology: A Review*, 1976-77: 72.

653. **Cunningham, A.**
Coins of ancient India from the earliest times down to the seventh century A.D. Varanasi, Indological Book House, 1963.

654. _____.
Coins of the Indo-Scythians, Sakas & Kushanas. Varanasi, Indological Book House, 1971.

655. **Dasgupta, Charu Chandra**
Ancient coins found in Pancala, Ayodhya, Kausambi and Mathura— a study. *Indian Historical Quarterly*, Vol. 8, No. 3, September 1933: 549-564.

656. **Dasgupta, Kalyan Kumar**
Indian coins and coin-symbols. *Journal of Ancient Indian History*, Vol. 14, 1983-84: 41-70.

657. _____.
A rare variety of Audumbara coins. *Indian Historical Quarterly*, Vol. 38, No. 1, March 1962: 76-79.

658. **Durga Prasad** and **Gupta, P.L.**
Clay-moulds of Punch-marked coins from Mathura. *Journal of the Numismatic Society of India*, Vol. 16, pt. 2, 1954: 166-176.

659. **Gupta, P.L.**
The coinage of the local kings of northern India and the date of Kaniska. In A.L. Basham, ed., *Papers on the date of Kaniska*. Leiden, E.J. Brill, 1968: 114-120.

660. _____.
Coins, New Delhi, National Book Trust, 1969.

661. _____.
Copper punch-marked coins from Sonkh. *Journal of the Numismatic Society of India*, Vol. 37, pts. 1-2, 1975: 1-2.

662. _____.
Early coins of Mathura region. In Dorris Meth Srinivasan, ed., *Mathura: The cultural heritage*. New Delhi, American Institute of Indian Studies, 1989: 124-139.

663. _____.
A Kushana coin with Brahmi legend. *Journal of the Numismatic Society of India*, Vol. 35, 1973: 123-126.

664. _____.
Some interesting coins from Sahet-Mahet. *Journal of the Numismatic Society of India*, Vol. 13, pt. 2, December 1951: 139-143.

665. **Hemmy, A.S.**
The weight standards of ancient Indian coins. *Journal of the Royal Asiatic Society of Great Britain and Ireland*, 1937: 1-26.

666. **Hodivala, S.H.**
Islamabad. *Journal and Proceedings of the Asiatic Society of Bengal*, New Series, Vol. 16, 1920: 194-197.

667. **Jayaswal, K.P.**
Some coins of the Mauryas and Sungas. *Journal of the Royal Asiatic Society of Great Britain and Ireland*, 1935: 788-792.

668. **Lahiri, Bela**
Observation on the coins of the Mitra rulers of Mathura. *Journal of the Numismatic Society of India*, Vol. 47, pts. 1-2, 1985: 100-105.

669. _____.
Problem of the so-called Mitra rulers of northern India. *Journal of the Numismatic Society of India*, Vol. 20, pt. 2, 1958: 123-143.

670. **Macdowall, D.W.**
The pattern of the Kusana copper coinage and the role of Mathura. In Doris Meth Srinivasan, ed., *Mathura: The cultural heritage*. New Delhi, American Institute of Indian Studies, 1989: 153-161.

671. **Maheshwari, K.K.** and **Wiggins, Kenneth W.**
Maratha mints and coinage. Nasik, Indian Institute of Research in Numismatic Studies, 1989.

672. **Maity, S.K.**
Early Indian coins and currency system. New Delhi, Munshiram Manoharlal, 1970.

673. Mathura Mitra coin, Mathura. *Indian Archaeological: A Review*, 1965-66: 78.

674. **Mitterwallner, Gritli Von**
Kusana coins and Kusana sculptures from Mathura. Mathura, Government Museum, 1986.

675. _____.
Legends of the "later" Kusana gold coins. *Numismatic Digest*, Vol. 10, 1986: 36-69.

676. **Mukherjee, B.N.**
The "Abhisheka of Lakshmi" motif on coins of the Mitra rulers of Mathura. *Journal of the Numismatic Society of India*, Vol. 39, pts. 1-2, 1977: 155-156.

677. _____.
An interesting coin from Sonkh, Mathura. *Journal of the Asiatic Society*, Vol. 15, 1973: 210-212.

678. _____.
A Kshatrapa of Mathura. *Journal of the Asiatic Society*, Vol. 19, 1977: 83-84.

679. _____.
Kushana coins of the land of the five rivers. Calcutta, Indian Museum, 1978.

680. _____.
Kushana silver coinage. Calcutta, Indian Museum, 1982.

681. _____.
Nana on lion: A study in Kushana numismatic art. Calcutta, The Asiatic Society, 1969.

682. _____.
Some aspects of the technique of minting Kushana coins. *Indian Museum Bulletin*, Vol. 18, 1983: 22-43.

683. **Nagar, M.M.**
Four new coins from Mathura. *Journal of the Numismatic Society of India*, Vol. 8, pt. 1, June 1946: 30-32.

684. **Narain, A.K.**
Ancient Mathura and the numismatic material. In Doris Meth Srinivasan, ed., *Mathura: The cultural heritage*. New Delhi, American Institute of Indian Studies, 1989: 115-118.

685. **Panna Lall**
A find of clay moulds for forging coins at Mathura. *Journal of the U.P. Historical Society*, Vol. 1, pt. 2, June 1918: 137-140.

686. **Rapson, E.J.**
Notes on Indian coins and seals. *Journal of the Royal Asiatic Society of Great Britain and Ireland*, 1900: 97-126.

687. _____.
Notes on Indian coins and seals. *Journal of the Royal Asiatic Society of Great Britain and Ireland*, 1900: 423-429.

688. _____.
Notes on Indian coins and seals. *Journal of the Royal Asiatic Society of Great Britain and Ireland*, 1901: 97-108.

689. _____.
Notes on Indian coins and seals. *Journal of the Royal Asiatic Society of Great Britain and Ireland*, 1903: 285-312.

690. _____.
Notes on Indian coins and seals. *Journal of the Royal Asiatic Society of Great Britain and Ireland*, 1905: 783-814.

691. **Ray, Sunil C.**
Stratigraphic evidence of coins from excavations at Mathura. In Doris Meth Srinivasan, ed., *Mathura: The cultural heritage*. New Delhi, American Institute of Indian Studies, 1989: 140-145.

692. _____.
Stratigraphic evidence of coins from excavations at Mathura. In K.K. Dasgupta and others, e.d., *Sraddhanjali; studies in ancient Indian history: D.C. Sircar commemoration volume*. Delhi, Sundeep Prakashan, 1988: 375-384.

693. **Sahi, M.D.N.**
Bearing of excavations on the chronology of Mathura coins. In A.K. Narain, ed., *Seminar papers on the local coins of Northern India, c. 300 B.C. to 300 A.D.* Varanasi, Department of Ancient Indian History, Culture & Archaeology, Banaras Hindu University, 1968: 62-66.

694. **Satya Prakash and Rajendra Singh**
Coinage in ancient India. New Delhi, The Research Institute of Ancient Scientific Studies, 1968.

695. **Satya Shrava**
The Kushana numismatics. New Delhi, Pranava Prakashan, 1985.

696. **Sharma, Savita**
Kusana mudraon me devi-devata. *Uttar Pradesh*, Vol. 11, No. 1, June 1982: 52-55. (Hindi)

697. **Singh, Arvind Kumar**
Mathura ke Mitra evam Dutt shasak. In Thakur Prasad Verma and others, ed., *Yugayugina Vraja*. Varanasi, Bharatiya Itihasa Samkalan Samiti, U.P., 1988: 49-55. (Hindi)

698. **Singh, Jai Prakash**
Study of local coin types of Mathura with particular reference to religious motifs. In Doris Meth Srinivasan, ed., *Mathura: The cultural heritage*. New Delhi, American Institute of Indian Studies, 1989: 146-152.

699. **Singh, Shatrughna Sharan**
Early coins of North India: An iconographic study. Patna, Janaki Prakashan, 1984.

700. **Sircar, D.C.**
Early Indian numismatic and epigraphical studies. Calcutta, Indian Museum, 1977.

701. _____.
Studies in Indian coins. Delhi, Motilal Banarsidass, 1968.

702. **Smith, Vincent Arthur**
The coinage of the early or Imperial Gupta dynasty of Northern India. *Journal of the Royal Asiatic Society of Great Britain and Ireland,* New Series, Vol. 21, 1889: 1-158.

703. _____.
Mathura, a mint of Akbar for copper coinage. *Indian Antiquary,* Vol. 38, 1909: 80.

704. **Sohoni, S.V.**
Uttamabhadra and king Uttamadatta of Mathura. *Journal of the Numismatic Society of India,* Vol. 7, 1945: 27-28.

705. **Srivastava, A.K.**
Coin hoards of Uttar Pradesh. Lucknow, The State Museum, 1980.

706. _____.
Mathura as known through the coins. *Bulletin of Museums and Archaeology in U.P.*, Nos. 11-12, June-December 1973: 30-36.

707. **Srivastava, Arvind Kumar**
Sikke. *Uttar Pradesh,* Vol. 8, No. 12, May 1981: 78-80, 87. (Hindi)

708. **Srivastava, A.K.**
Treasure trove finds from Mathura. In Doris Meth Srinivasan, ed., *Mathura: The cultural heritage.* New Delhi, American Institute of Indian Studies, 1989: 119-123.

709. _____.
Treasure trove finds from Mathura district. *Bulletin of Museums and Archaeology in U.P.*, Nos. 11-12, June-December 1973: 37-41.

710. **Srivastava, A.L.**
Srivatsa symbol on early Indian coins. *Bulletin of Museums and Archaeology in U.P.*, No. 14, December 1974: 5-13.

711. **Srivastava, C.S.**
Kusana hoards of treasure trove coins from Uttar Pradesh (1941-42 to 1969-70). *Bulletin of Museums and Archaeology in U.P.*, No. 3, June 1969: 48-67.

712. **Thaplyal, Kiran Kumar**
Studies in ancient Indian seals. Lucknow, Akhila Bharatiya Sanskrit Parishad, 1972.

713. **Theobald, W.**
Notes on early local silver coinage in North-Western India and in the Konkan. *Journal of the Asiatic Society of Bengal*, Vol. 63, pt. 1, No. 2, 1894: 73-84.

714. **Vanaja, R.**
History of the Mitra kings from numismatic and epigraphic evidence. In Pushpendra Kumar, ed., *India in Sanskrit inscriptions*. Delhi, Nag Publishers, 1986: 8-24.

715. **Walsh, E.H.C.**
Punch-marked silver coins; Their standard of weight, age and minting. *Journal of the Royal Asiatic Society of Great Britain and Ireland*, 1937: 293-304.

ART, ICONOGRAPHY AND SCULPTURE

716. **Agrawal, O.P.**
Conservation problem of Mathura sculptures. *Journal of Indian Museums*, Vol. 29, 1973: 43-49.

717. **Agrawala, P.K.**
Early Indian bronzes. Varanasi, Prithivi Prakshan, 1977.

718. _____.
Mathura railing pillars. Varanasi, Prithivi Prakashan, 1966.

719. **Agrawala, R.C.**
Carved pillar of Gupta year 61. *Journal of the Oriental Institute*, Vol. 19, No. 4, June 1970: 355-356.

720. _____.
More sculptures from the National Museum, New Delhi. *East and West*, New Series, Vol. 20, No. 3, September 1970: 351-355.

721. _____.
Some Kusana sculptures in the National Museum, Delhi and allied problems. *Bulletin of Museums and Archaeology in U.P.*, No. 3, June 1969: 6-24.

722. _____.
Unpublished sculptures and terracottas in the National Museum, New Delhi, and some allied problems. *East and West*, New Series, Vol. 17, Nos. 3-4, September-December 1967: 276-286.

723. **Agrawala, V.S.**
Architectural pieces in Mathura Museum. Varanasi, Prithivi Prakashan, 1963.

724. _____.
Astamangalakamala. *Journal of the Indian Society of Oriental Art*, New Series, Vol. 2, 1967-1968: 1-3.

725. _____.
Bharatiya kala. Varanasi, Prithivi Prakashan, 1977. (Hindi)

726. _____.
Catalogue of the Mathura Museum. *Journal of the U.P. Historical Society*, Vol. 23, pts. 1-2, 1950: 35-147.

727. _____.
Catalogue of the Mathura Museum: Architectural pieces. *Journal of the U.P. Historical Society*, Vols. 24-25, 1951-1952: 1-160.

728. _____.
Evolution of the Hindu temple and other essays. Varanasi, Prithivi Prakashan, 1979.

729. _____.
Further acquisitions to the Mathura Museum. *Journal of the U.P. Historical Society*, Vol. 10, pt. 1, July 1937: 88-90.

730. _____.
Gupta art. Varanasi, Prithivi Prakashan, 1977.

731. _____.
Gupta art. *Journal of the U.P. Historical Society*, Vol. 18, 1945: 101-134.

732. _____.
Handbook of the sculptures in the Curzon Museum of Archaeology, Muttra. Allahabad, Printing and Stationery, U.P., 1939.

733. _____.
The heritage of Indian art. New Delhi, Publications Division, 1964.

734. _____.
India—a nation. Varanasi, Prithivi Prakashan, 1983.

735. _____.
Indian art: A history of Indian art from the earliest times up to the third century A.D. Varanasi, Prithivi Prakashan, 1965.

736. _____.
Indian sculpture—a cultural saga. *Roopa-Lekha*, Vol. 20, No. 1, 1948: I-V.

737. _____.
Masterpieces of Mathura sculpture. Varanasi, Prithivi Prakashan, 1965.

738. _____.
Mathura-kala. Ahmedabad, Gujarat Vidyasabha, 1964.(Hindi)

739. _____.
Mathura-kala. In V.S. Agrawala, ed., *Seth Kanhaiya Lal Poddar abhinandana grantha*. Mathura, Akhila Bharatiya Braj Sahitya Mandal, 1953: 783-798. (Hindi)

740. _____.
Mathura railing pillars. *Roopa-Lekha*, Vol. 2, No. 3, 1940: 14-18.

741. _____.
New sculptures from Mathura. *Journal of the U.P. Historical Society*, Vol. 11, pt. 2, December 1938: 66-76.

742. _____.
A new stone umbrella from Mathura. *Journal of the U.P. Historical Society*, Vol. 20, pts. 1-2, July-December 1947: 65-67.

743. _____.
Palace-scenes on a Mathura pillar in the Lucknow Museum. *Journal of the U.P. Historical Society*, Vol. 19, pts. 1-2; July-December 1946: 56-60.

744. _____.
Pre-Kushana art of Mathura. Varanasi, Prithivi Prakashan, 1984.

745. **Agrawala, V.S.** and **Upadhya, B.S.**
A relief of Rsya Sranga in the Mathura Museum. *Journal of the Indian Society of Oriental Art*, Vol. 4, No. 1, June 1936: 62-64.

746. **Agrawala, V.S.**
A short guide-book to the archaeological section of the Provincial Museum, Lucknow. Allahabad, Printing and Stationery, U.P., 1940.

747. _____.
Studies in Indian art. Varanasi, Vishwavidyalaya Prakashan, 1965.

748. _____.
The vine motif in Mathura art. *Journal of the Indian Society of Oriental Art*, Vol. 4, No. 2, December 1936: 130-133.

749. _____.
The wheel flag of India: Chakra-dhvaja. Varanasi, Prithivi Prakashan, 1964.

750. **Andeson, John**
Catelogue and handbook of the archaeological collections in the Indian Museum. Calcutta, Indian Museum, 1883. 2 parts.

751. **Archer, W.G.**
Sir William Rothenstein and Indian art. *Art and Letters*, New Series, Vol. 25, No. 1, 1951: 1-7.

752. Art of India: Stone sculpture. New York, The Asia Society, 1962.

753. **Asher, Frederick M.**
The art of Eastern India, 300-800. Minneapolis, The University of Minnesota Press, 1980.

754. **Ashton, Leigh,** ed.
The art of India and Pakistan: A commemorative catalogue of the exhibition held at the Royal Academy of Arts, London, 1947-8. London, Faber and Faber, 1949.

755. **Asthana, Shashi**
The Kushana art of Mathura. In S.P. Gupta, ed., *Kushana sculptures from Sanghol (1st-2nd century A.D): recent discovery*. New Delhi, National Museum, 1985: 25-36.

756. **Auboyer, Jeannine**
Indian sculpture, *Burlington Magazine*, Vol. 90, February 1948: 37-40.

757. **Bachhofer, Ludwig**
Die Hariti von Sparah Dheri. *Ostasiatische Zeitschrift*, 1936: 100-107. (German)

758. _____.
Early Indian sculpture. New Delhi, Munshiram Manoharlal, 1973.

759. _____.
Zur ara Kanishkas. *Ostasiatische Zeitschrift*, 1930: 10-15. (German)

760. **Bajpai, K.D.**
Braj ki kala. Mathura, Deshbanhu Pustakalaya, 1959. (Hindi)

761. _____.
The Kusana art of Mathura. *Marg*, Vol. 15, No. 2, March 1962: 28-42.

762. _____.
Mathura ke vedikastambha. *Kala-Nidhi*, Vol. 1, No. 4: 41-44. (Hindi).

763. _____.
Mathura ki pracheen kala me samanvaya bhavana. In *Chotte Lal Jain Smriti granth.* Calcutta, Babu Chotte Lal Jain Abhinandan Samiti, 1967: 107-110 (Hindi)

764. _____.
New acquisitions to the Mathura Museum. *Journal of Indian Musuems,* Vol. 10, 1954: 31-32.

765. _____.
A note on some newly discovered sculptures in U.P *Journal of Indian Museums,* Vol. 8, 1952: 47-48.

766. _____.
Religious background of ancient Indian art. *Puratan,* Vol. 1, 1984: 1-6.

767. _____.
Some problems of the Kushana art. *Journal of the U.P. Historical Society,* New Series, Vol. 9, pt. 1, 1961: 1-5.

768. _____.
A unique stone head from Mathura. *Jaina Antiquary,* Vol. 22, No. 1, December 1963: 32.

769. _____.
Uttar Pradesh ke sanskritik kendra: Mathura. Lucknow, Shikha Vibhag, U.P., 1955. (Hindi)

770. _____.
Uttar Pradesh ki eithasik vibhuti. Lucknow, Shikha Vibhag, U.P., 1957. (Hindi).

771. _____.
Woman plucking flowers. *Lalit Kala,* Nos.1-2: 80.

772. _____.
Yug-yugo me Uttar Pradesh. Allahabad, Shiksha Vibhag, U.P., 1955. (Hindi)

773. **Baktay, Ervin**
Die Kunst Indiens. Budapest, Akademiai Kiado, 1965. (German)

774. **Bandyopadhyay, Bimal**
Survey of Indian metal sculpture. Delhi, Sundeep Prakashan, 1987.

775. **Banerji, R.D.**
Three sculptures in the Lucknow Museum. *Archaeological Survey of India Annual Report,* 1909-10: 146-149.

776. **Bartholomew, Terese Tse**
The arts of India and Lamaist countries. *Oriental Art,* New Series, Vol. 22, No. 4, 1976: 391-395.

777. **Bharatha Iyer, K.**
Animals in Indian sculpture. Bombay, D.B. Taraporevala Sons & Co., 1977.

778. **Bhattacharya, S.K.**
The story of Indian art. Delhi, Atma Ram & Sons, 1966.

779. **Bhattacharyya, Benoytosh**
Statue of Castana. *Journal of the Bihar and Orissa Research Society,* Vol. 6, pt. 1, March 1920: 51-53.

780. **Biswas, T.K.** and **Jha, Bhogendra**
Gupta sculptures (in) Bharat Kala Bhavan. New Delhi, Books & Books, 1985.

781. **Biswas, T.K.**
Horse in early Indian art. New Delhi, Munshiram Manoharlal, 1987.

782. **Bussagli, Mario** and **Sivaramaurti, C.**
5000 years of the art of India. New York, Harry N. Abrams, (n.d.).

783. **Chanda, Ramaprasad**
The Mathura School of sculpture. *Archaeological Survey of India Annual Report,* 1922-23: 164-170.

784. _____.
The Mathura School of sculpture. *Indian Museum Bulletin,* Vol. 10, No. 1, January 1975: 35-40.

785. _____.
Medieval Indian sculpture. *Archaeological Survey of India Annual Report,* 1929-30: 215-221.

786. _____.
Medieval sculpture in Eastern India. *Indian Museum Bulletin,* Vol. 11, No. 2, July 1976: 7-16.

787. _____.
Medieval sculpture in Eastern India. *Journal of the Department of Letters,* Vol. 3: 225-246.

788. **Chaturvedi, H.K.**
Mathura sculptures in the National Museum. *Bulletin of Museums and Archaeology in U.P.,* No. 14, December 1974: 23-35.

789. **Codrington, K. De B.**
Ancient India. London, Ernest Benn, 1926.

790. _____.
Sculpture. In Leigh Aston, ed., *The Art of India and Pakistan*. London, Faber and Faber, 1950: 3-84.

791. **Coomaraswamy, A.K.**
Catalogue of the Indian collections in the Museum of Fine Arts, Boston. Boston, Museum of Fine Arts, 1923. Pts. 1-2.

792. _____.
Early Indian sculptures: Six reliefs from Mathura. *Bulletin of the Museum of Fine Arts, Boston*, Vol. 24, No. 144, August 1926: 54-60.

793. _____.
History of Indian and Indonesian art. New York, Dover Publications, 1965.

794. _____.
Introduction to Indian art. Delhi, Munshiram Manoharlal, 1969.

795. _____.
Portfolio of Indian art objects selected from the collections of the Museum of Fine Arts, Boston. New York, E. Weyhe, 1923.

796. **Craven, Roy C.**
A concise history of Indian art. New Delhi, Vikas Publishing House, 1979.

797. **Craven, Roy C., Jr.**
Indian sculpture in the John and Mable Ringline Museum of Art. Florida, University of Florida Press, 1961.

798. **Czuma, Stanislaw**
Indian art from the George P. Bickford collection. Cleveland, Cleveland Museum of Art, 1975.

799. _____.
Kushan sculpture: Images from early India. In *Festival of India in the United States, 1985-1986*. New York, Harry N. Abrams, 1985: 19-22.

800. _____.
Kushan sculpture: Images from early India. Cleveland, Cleveland Museum of Art, 1985.

801. **Davidson, J. Le Roy**
Art of the Indian subcontinent from Los Angeles collections. Los Angeles, University of California, 1968.

802. _____.
Mannerism and neurosis in the erotic art of India. *Oriental Art*, New Series, Vol. 6, No. 3, 1960: 83-90.

803. **Deneck, M.M.**
Indian sculpture: Masterpieces of Indian Khmer and Cham art. London, Spring Books, 1962.

804. **Desai, Devangana**
Erotic sculpture of India : A socio-cultural study. New Delhi, Munshiram Manoharlal, 1985.

805. Devata holding a Chauri. Cleveland Museum of Art, Cleveland *Archives of Asian Art*, Vol. 20, 1966-1967: 87.

806. **Dhavalikar, M.K.**
Early Indian art and the cultural pattern. *Journal of the Indian Society of Oriental Art*, New Series, Vol. 8, 1976-1977: 69-75.

807. _____.
Mathura art in the Baroda Museum. Baroda, Department of Museums, 1970.

808. **Dwivedi, Radhey Shyam**
Braj Ki murti kala. In Radhey Shyam Dwivedi, ed., *Braj Vaibhav*. Mathura, Bharati Anusandhan Bhawan, 1972: 181-182. (Hindi)

809. **Dwivedi, V.P.**
Mathura art in the Museums of United States of America. *Journal of Indian Museums*, Vol. 29, 1973: 22-29.

810. Exhibition of art chiefly from the dominions of India & Pakistan, Royal Academy of Arts, London, 1947-48. London, Country Life Limited, 1947.

811. **Fabri, Charles L.**
Discovering Indian sculpture: A brief history. New Delhi, Affiliated East-West Press, 1970.

812. _____.
Mathura of the Gods. *Marg*, Vol. 7, No. 2: 8-22.

813. _____.
Two notes on Indian head-dress. *Journal of the Royal Asiatic Society of Great Britain and Ireland*, 1931: 597-601.

814. **Foucher, A.**
On an old bas-relief in the Museum at Mathura. *Journal of the Bihar and Orissa Research Society*, Vol. 6, pt. 4, December 1920: 470-473.

815. _____.
Ancient female statue from Mathura. *Technical Art Series*, 1897: Plate 1.

816. **Gangoly, O.C.**
A brass statuette from Mathura. *Rupam*, No. 2, April 1920: 1-3.

817. _____.
A Kusana caryatid from Mathura. *Rupam*, No. 31, July 1927: 73-74.

818. _____.
A new museum of Indian art at Benares. *Indian Art and Letters*, New Series, Vol. 5, No. 1, 1931: 9-13.

819. **Growse, F.S.**
Supposed Greek sculpture at Mathura. *Journal of the Asiatic Society of Bengal*, Vol. 44, pt. 1, No. 3, 1875: 212-215.

820. A guide to the galleries of the National Museum of India. New Delhi, National Museum, 1956.

821. **Gunasinghe, Siri**
La forme feminine dans la sculpture pre-Gupta. *Arts Asiatiques*, Vol. 3, No. 2, 1956: 98-123.

822. **Gupta, S.P.**, ed.
Kushana sculptures from Sanghol (1st-2nd century A.D.): A recent discovery. New Delhi, National Museum, 1985. Vol. 1.

823. _____.
Masterpieces from the National Museum collection. New Delhi, National Museum, 1985.

824. _____.
The roots of Indian art. Delhi, B.R. Publishing Corporation, 1980.

825. _____.
Sanghol: The meeting place of works of art of Gandhara and Mathura schools. In *Investigating Indian art*. Berlin, Staatliche Museen Preussischer Kulturbesitz, 1987: 89-104.

826. **Hallade, Madeleine**
Mathura. In *Encyclopedia of World Art*, Vol. 9. New York, McGraw-Hill Book Company, 1964: 579-586.

827. **Handa, Devendra**
A Kusana portrait statue from Punjab. *Bulletin of Museums and Archaeology in U.P.*, No. 37, June 1986: 1-2.

828. **Hari Dutt Shastri**
Kusana yug ki murtikala. In Radhey Shyam Dwivedi, ed., *Braj Vaibhav*. Mathura, Bharati Anusandhan Bhawan, 1972: 79-80. (Hindi)

829. **Harle, J.C.**
The art and architecture of the Indian subcontinent. Middlesex. Penguin Books, 1986.

830. _____.
Gupta sculpture: Indian sculpture of the fourth to the sixth centuries A.D. Oxford, Clarendon Press, 1974.

831. **Harle, J.C.** and **Topsfield, Andrew**
Indian art in the Ashmolean Museum. Oxford, Ashmolean Museum, 1987.

832. **Harle, J.C.**
Late Kusan, early Gupta: A reverse approach. In Norman Hammond, ed., *South Asian archaeology: Papers from the First International Conference of South Asian Archaeologists held in the University of Cambridge*. London, Gerald Duckworth & Co., 1973: 231-240.

833. _____.
Mathura sculpture in the Ashmolean Museum. *Bulletin of Museums and Archaeology in U.P.*, Nos. 15-16, June-December 1975: 15-17.

834. **Hartel, Herbert** and **Auboyer, Jeannine**
Indien und Sudostasien. Berlin, Propylaen Verlag, 1971. (German)

835. **Hartel, Herbert**
Indische skulpturen. Berlin, Museum fur Volkerkunde, 1960. (German)

836. **Hartel, Herbert** and **Lobo, Wibke**
Schatze Indischer kunst. Berlin, Staaiche Museen Preussischer Kulturbesitz, Museum fur Indische Kunst, 1984. (German)

837. **Havell, E.B.**
The art heritage of India. Bombay, D.B. Taraporevala Sons & Co., 1964.

838. _____.
A handbook of Indian art. Varanasi, Indic Academy, 1972.

839. **Heeramaneck, Alice N.**
Masterpieces of Indian sculpture from the former collections of Nasli M. Heeramaneck. U.S.A., The author, 1979.

840. **Horvath, Vera**
Mathura art in the Francis Hopp Museum in Budapest. *Bulletin of Museums and Archaeology in U.P.*, No. 14, December 1974: 19-22.

841. **Huntington, Susan L.**
The art of ancient India. New York, John Weatherhill, 1985.

842. **Irwin, John**
Indian art through western eyes. *Times of India Annual*, 1949: 13-18.

843. **Joshi, N.P.**
Bharatiya murtishastra. Nagpur, M.U.B.P. Board, 1979. (Marathi)

844. **Joshi, N.P.** and **Sharma, R.C.**
Catalogue of Gandhara sculptures in the State Museum, Lucknow. Lucknow, The State Museum, 1969.

845. **Joshi, N.P.**
Harivamṣa ke kuchh Kusana kaleen shalok. *Bulletin of Museums and Archaeology in U.P.*, No. 8, December 1971: 1-10. (Hindi)

846. _____.
Kuchḥ aprakashit kalakratiyan. *Bulletin of Museums and Archaeology in U.P.*, No. 4, December 1969: 9-18. (Hindi)

847. _____.
Mathura kala me manglik chinha. In *Pt. Suratinarayana Mani Tripathi abhinandana grantha.* Varanasi, Pt. Suratinarayana Mani Tripathi Abhinandana Samiti, 1965: 32-37. (Hindi)

848. _____.
Mathura ki murtikala. Mathura, Mathura Sangrahalaya, 1965. (Hindi)

849. _____.
Mathura sculptures. Mathura, Archaeological Museum, 1966.

850. _____.
Pracheen Bharatiya murtivijnana. Patna, Bihar Rashtrabhasha Parishad, 1977. (Hindi)

851. _____.
Some Kusana passages in the Harivamsa. In Herbert Hartel and Volkar Moeller, ed., *Indologantagung* 1971. Wiesbaden, Franz Steiner Verlag GMBH, 1973: 238-252.

852. _____.
Shri Krsna-janmasthan, Mathura ka pracheen murti sangraha. *Sri Krisna Sandesh*, Vol. 2, No. 1, 1966: 109-112.

853. _____.
Use of auspicious symbols in the Kusana art at Mathura. In G.T. Deshpande and others, ed., *Felicitation volume: A collection of forty-two Indological essays presented to Dr. V.V. Mirashi*. Nagpur, Vidarbha Samshodhan Mandal, 1965: 311-317.

854. **Kala, Jayantika**
Epic scenes in Indian plastic art. New Delhi, Abhinav Publications, 1988.

855. **Kar, Chintamoni**
Classical Indian sculpture, 300 B.C. to A.D. 500. London, Alec Tiranti Ltd., 1950.

856. **Khandalavala, Karl** and **Roy, Archana**
Sculpture. *Marg*, Vol. 38, No. 3: 9-38.

857. _____.
Sculpture. In Karl Khandalavala and Saryu Doshi, ed., *A Collector's dream*. Bombay, Marg Publications, 1987: 9-38.

858. **Kieffer, C.M.**
Kusana art and the historic effigies of Mat (India) and Surkh Kotal (Afghanistan). *Marg*, Vol. 15, No. 2, March 1962: 43-48.

859. **Kramrisch, Stella**
The art of India. London, The Phaidon Press, 1965.

860. _____.
Figural sculpture of the Gupta period. In Barbara Stoler Miller, ed., *Exploring India's art: Selected writings of Stella Kramrisch.* Philadelphia, University of Pennsylvania Press, 1983: 181-203.

861. _____.
Indian sculpture. Calcutta, Y.M.C.A. Publishing House, 1933.

862. _____.
Indian sculpture in the Philadelphia Museum of Art. Philadelphia, University of Pennsylvania Press, 1960.

863. _____.
Madhupana scenes from Mathura, etc. *Journal of the Indian Society of Oriental Art*, Vol. 6, 1938: 197-200.

864. **Krishna Kumar**
The evidence of white-wash, plaster and pigment on North Indian sculpture with special reference to Sarnath. *Artibus Asiae*, Vol. 45, 1984: 199-206.

865. **Krishna Murthy, K.**
Mythical animals in Indian art. New Delhi, Abhinav Publications, 1985.

866. Kushan sculpture, Jaitpur, district Mathura. *Indian Archaeology: A Review*, 1961-62: 104.

867. **Larson, Gerald James, Pal, Pratapạditya and Gowen, Rebecca P.**
In her image: The great goddess in Indian Asia and the Madonna in Christian culture. Santa Barbara, U.C.S.B. Art Museum, 1980.

868. **Lohuizen-De Leeuw, J.E. Van**
The date of Kaniska and some recently published images. In A.L. Basham, ed., *Papers on the date of Kaniska.* Leiden, E.J. Brill, 1968: 126-133.

869. _____.
Gandhara and Mathura: Their cultural relationship. In Pratapaditya Pal, ed., *Aspects of Indian art: Papers presented in a symposium at the Los Angeles County Museum of Art, October 1970.* Leiden, E.J. Brill, 1972: 27-43.

870. _____.
Heinrich Zimmer and Indian art. *Arts Asiatiques*, Vol. 4, No. 3, 1957: 221-235. (French)

871. _____.
Oriental treasures in Amsterdam. *Oriental Art*, New Series, Vol. 1, No. 1, 1955: 13-16.

872. _____.
The "Scythian period". Leiden, E.J. Brill, 1949.

873. _____.
Two notes on Mathura scultpure. In *India Antiqua, A volume of Oriental Studies presented by his friends and pupils to Jean Philippe Vogel on the occasion of the fiftieth anniversary of his doctorate*. Leiden, E.J. Brill, 1947: 231-239.

874. **Mahmud, Mohammad Khalid**
The sculpture portrait of king Kanishka. *Oriental Art*, New Series, Vol. 30, No. 4, 1984/85: 371-378.

875. **Marshall, J.H.**
Archaeological exploration in India, 1909-10. *Journal of the Royal Asiatic Society of Great Britain and Ireland*, 1911: 127-158.

876. **Mathur, N.L.**
Sculpture in India; its history & art. New Delhi, The author, 1972.

877. **Mehta, Rustam J.**
Masterpieces of Indian sculpture. Bombay, D.B. Taraporevala Sons & Co., 1976.

878. _____.
Masterpieces of the female form in Indian art. Bombay, D.B. Taraporevala Sons & Co., 1972.

879. **Meister, Michael W.**
The arts of India and Nepal: The Nasli and Alice Heeramaneck collection. *Oriental Art*, New Series, Vol. 14, No. 2, 1968: 107-113.

880. **Michell, George**, ed.
In the image of man: The Indian perception of the universe through 2000 years of painting and sculpture. London, Arts Council of Great Britain, 1982.

881. **Misra, Shivadhar**
New acquisitions (April 1963-March 1965), Archaeological Museum, Mathura. *Bulletin of Museums and Archaeology in U.P.*, No. 1, March 1968: 62-65.

882. **Mittal, Prabhu Dayal**
Braj ki kalaon ka itihas. Mathura, Sahitya Sansthan, 1975. (Hindi)

883. **Mookerji, Radha Kumud**
Notes on early Indian art. *Journal of the U.P. Historical Society*, Vol. 12, pt. 1, July 1939: 49-82.

884. **Moore, Albert C.**
Iconography of religions: An introduction. London, S.C.M. Press, 1977.

885. **Morley, Grace**
Indian sculpture. Varanasi, Lustre Press Pvt. Ltd., 1985.

886. **Moti Chandra**, ed.
Seminar on Indian art history. New Delhi, Lalit Kala Akademi, 1962.

887. ____.
Stone sculpture in the Prince of Wales Museum. Bombay, Prince of Wales Museum of Western India, 1974.

888. **Mukherjee, B.N.**
Problems of dated images of the Mathura School of sculpture of the Kushan period. In *Central Asia in the Kushan period: Proceedings of the International Conference of the History, Archaeology and Culture of Central Asia in the Kushan period, 1968*, Vol. 2, UNESCO, 1975: 346-362.

889. **Mukhopadhyay, Mihir Mohan**
A fragmentary sculpture of a female from Mathura. *Indian History Congress, Proceedings*, Session 28, 1966: 23-24.

890. ____.
Kalyanasundara theme in North Indian art. *Journal of the Indian Society of Oriental Art*, New Series, Vol. 2, 1967-1968: 4-15.

891. ____.
Sculptures of Ganga-Yamuna valley. New Delhi, Abhniav Publications, 1984.

892. **Munshi, K.M.**
Indian temple sculpture. Calcutta, Rupa & Co., 1959.

893. **Nagar, M.M.**
A new Indo-Scythian head from Mathura. *Journal of the U.P. Historical Society*, Vol. 13, pt. 1, July 1940: 51.

894. _____.
Some newly acquired antiquities in the Mathura Museum. *Journal of the U.P. Historical Society*, Vol. 12, pt. 2, December 1939: 49-51.

895. _____.
Two Garuda images in Mathura Museum. *Journal of the Bihar and Orissa Research Society*, Vol. 28, pt. 4, December 1942: 468-472.

896. **Nehru, Lolita**
The narrative reliefs from Gandhara and Mathura of the Kushana period: A broad comparison. In Amita Ray and others, ed., *Indian Studies: Essays presented in memory of Prof. Niharranjan Ray*. Delhi, Caxton Publications, (n.d.): 341-345.

897. **Pal, Pratapaditya**
The ideal image: The Gupta sculptural tradition and its influence. New York, The Asia Society, 1978.

898. _____.
Indian sculpture. *Arts of Asia*, Vol. 15, No. 6, November-December 1985: 68-79.

899. _____.
Indian sculpture: A catalogue of the Los Angeles County Museum of Art collection. Los Angeles, Los Angeles County Museum of Art, 1986, Vol. 1, Circa 500 B.C.-A.D. 700.

900. _____.
A Kusana bronze from Mathura. *Journal of Ancient Indian History*, Vol. 15, pts. 1-2, 1985-1986: 224-228.

901. _____.
The sensuous immortals: A selection of the sculptures from the Pan-Asian collection. Los Angeles, Los Angeles County Museum of Art, (1978).

902. **Pathak, Indu Mati**
Some interesting images of Patna Museum. *Journal of the Bihar Research Society*, Vol. 61, 1975: 92-96.

903. **Pope, John**
An exhibition of the sculpture of Greater India: A fully illustrated catalogue. New York, C.T. Loo & Co., 1942.

904. Portfolio. *Marg*, Vol. 15, No. 2, March 1962: 17-26.

905. **Postel, M.**
Ear ornaments of ancient India. Bombay, Franco-Indian Pharmaceuticals, 1989.

906. **Prakash, Pratibha**
Pracheen mranaymurti kala. *Uttar Pradesh*, Vol. 9, No. 12, May 1981: 68-71. (Hindi)

907. **Pramod Chandra**
The sculpture and architecture of Northern India. In Basil Gray, ed., *The arts of India*. Oxford, Phaidon Press, 1981: 30-52.

908. _____.
Stone sculpture in the Allahabad Museum. New Delhi, American Institute of Indian Studies, 1970.

909. **Randhawa, M.S.**
The cult of trees and tree worship in Buddhist-Hindu sculpture. *Roopa-Lekha*, Vol. 33: 1-42.

910. _____.
The cult of trees and tree worship in Buddhist-Hindu sculpture. New Delhi, All India Fine Arts & Crafts Society, 1964.

911. **Randhawa, Mohinder Singh** and **Randhawa, Doris Schreier**
Indian sculpture; the scene, themes and legends. Bombay, Vakils, Feffer & Simons, 1985.

912. Rare sculptures: Selections from some Indian Museums exhibited in Japan. New Delhi, National Museum, 1984.

913. **Ray, Niharranjan**
An approach to Indian art. Chandigarh, Panjab University, 1974.

914. _____.
Idea and image in Indian art. New Delhi, Munshiram Manoharlal, 1973.

915. _____.
Maurya and post-Maurya art. New Delhi, Indian Council of Historical Research, 1975.

916. _____.
Maurya and Sunga art. Calcutta, Indian Studies: Past & Present, 1965.

917. Red sandstone railing pillar. *British Museum Quarterly*, Vol. 30, Nos. 1-2, 1965: 64.

918. **Rosenfield, John M.**
The dynastic arts of the Kushans. Berkeley and Los Angeles, University of California Press, 1967.

919. _____.
The Mathura School of sculpture; two contributions to the study of Kushan chronology. In A.L. Basham, ed., *Papers on the date of Kaniska submitted to the Conference on the date of Kaniska*, London, 20-22 April, 1960. Leiden, E.J. Brill, 1968: 259-277.

920. **Rowland, Benjamin**
The art and architecture of India: Buddhist, Hindu, Jain. Middlesex, Penguin Books Ltd., 1956.

921. _____.
Gandhara, Rome and Mathura: The early relief style. *Archives of the Chinese Art Society of America*, Vol. 10, 1956: 8-17.

922. **Sahni, Daya Ram**
Catalogue of the Museum of Archaeology at Sarnath. Calcutta, Government Printing, 1914.

923. **Saraswati, S.K.**
A survey of Indian sculpture. Calcutta, Firma K.L. Mukhopadhyay, 1957.

924. Sculptures. *Annual progress report of the Superintendent, Archaeological Survey, Hindu and Buddhist monuments, Northern Circle for the year ending 31st March 1921*: 27.

925. **Shanti, Swarup**
5000 years of arts and crafts in India and Pakistan. Bombay, D.B. Taraporevala Sons & Co., 1968.

926. **Sharma, B.N.**
The enduring charm of Gupta sculptures. *Roopa-Lekha*, Vol. 52, 1981: 28-38.

927. _____.
Indian art through the ages: A Panoramic view. *Vishveshvaranand Indological Journal*, Vol. 9, pt. 2, September 1971: 391-397.

928. _____.
Ravana lifting mount Kailasa in Indian art. *East and West*, New Series, Vol. 23, Nos. 3-4, September-December 1973: 327-338.

929. **Sharma, R.C.**
Album of art treasures: Mathura sculptures. Calcutta, Indian Museum, 1987.

930. _____.
Braj ki sajja kala. *Bulletin of Museums and Archaeology in U.P.*, No. 26, December 1980: 59-64. (Hindi)

931. _____.
Gupta sculpture from Mathura. *Bulletin of Museums and Archaeology in U.P.*, Nos. 27-28: June-December 1981; 89-109.

932. **Sharma, R.C. and Misra, Shivadhar**
Kusana acquisitions in the Mathura Museum during the last decade. *Bulletin of Museums and Archaeology in U.P.*, No. 4, December 1969: 46-65.

933. **Sharma, R.C.**
Kusana idiom in Mathura. In D.C. Bhattacharyya and Devendra Handa, ed., *Praci-prabha; perspectives in Indology: Essays in honour of Professor B.N. Mukherjee*. New Delhi, Harman Publishing House, 1980: 225-233.

934. _____.
Mathura as school of sculpture. In Lokesh Chandra and others, ed., *Dimensions of Indian art: Pupul Jayakar seventy*, Vol. 1, Delhi, Agam Kala Prakashan, 1986: 407-416.

935. _____.
Mathura kala shaili ki anuthi den. *Bulletin of Museums and Archaeology in U.P.*, Nos. 11-12, June-December 1973: 21-29. (Hindi)

936. _____.
Mathura ki murtikala. *Uttar Pradesh*, Vol. 9, No. 12, May 1981: 25-29. (Hindi)

937. _____.
Mathura Museum and art. Second edition. Mathura, Government Museum, 1976.

938. _____.
New art treasures from Mathura. *National Museum Bulletin*, Nos. 4-6: 39-43.

939. _____.
New rare sculptures in Mathura Museum. *Bulletin of Museums and Archaeology in U.P.*, No. 8, December 1971: 71-75.

940. **Siddiqi, W.H.**
Two newly discovered pre-Kusana sculptures from Rsikesa (Uttar Pradesh). *Journal of the Indian Society of Oriental Art*, Special Number, 1978: 76-80.

941. **Singh, Sheo Bahadur**
Syncretic icons in Uttar Pradesh. *East and West*, New Series, Vol. 23, Nos. 3-4, September-December 1973: 339-346.

942. **Sinha, Binod Chandra**
Tree worship in ancient India. New Delhi, Books Today, 1979.

943. **Sinha, Narendra Kumar**
A rare Mathura-head in the Bharatiya Kala Bhawan, Gaya. In B.N. Mukherjee and others, ed., *Sri Dinesacandrika; Studies in Indology: Shri D.C. Sircar Festschrift*. Delhi, Sundeep Prakashan, 1983: 401.

944. **Sivaramamurti, C.**
An album of Indian sculpture. New Delhi, National Book Trust, 1975.

945. _____.
The art of India. New York, Harry N. Abrams, 1977.

946. _____.
Birds and animals in Indian sculpture. New Delhi, National Museum, 1974.

947. _____.
Indian sculpture. Bombay, Allied Publishers, 1961.

948. _____.
Invitation to Indian art. New Delhi, Arnold-Heinemann, 1985.

949. _____.
Masterpieces of Indian sculpture in the National Museum New Delhi, National Museum, 1971.

950. _____.
Sanskrit literature and art-mirrors of Indian culture. New Delhi, Lakshmi Book Store, 1970. (Memoirs of the Archaeological Survey of India, No. 73).

951. _____.
Sculpture inspired by Kalidasa. New Delhi, Kanak Publications, 1984.

952. **Smith, Vincent A.**
Graeco-Roman influence on the civilization of ancient India. *Journal of the Asiatic Society of Bengal*, Vol. 58, pt. 1, No. 3, 1889: 107-198.

953. _____.
A history of fine art in India & Ceylon. Bombay, D.B. Taraporevala Sons & Co., (n.d.)

954. **Spagnoli, Maria Mariottini**
Some further observations on the symbolic meaning of the club in the statue of Kaniska. *East and West*, New Series, Vol. 20, No. 4, December 1970: 460-468.

955. _____.
The symbolic meaning of the club in the iconography of the Kusana kings. *East and West*, New Series, Vol. 17, Nos. 3-4, September-December 1967: 248-267.

956. **Srivastava, A.K.** and **Shukla, Sri Ranjan**
Master pieces in the Mathura Museum. *Bulletin of Museums and Archaeology in U.P.*, Nos. 19-20, June-December 1977: 75-81.

957. **Srivastava, Arvind Kumar**
Rajkiya Samgrahalaya Mathura me krsna kathanak kalakratiyan—ek survekshan. *Bulletin of Museums and Archaeology in U.P.*, Nos. 21-24, June 1978-December 1979: 127-137. (Hindi)

958. **Srivastava, A.L.**
Mathura: The cradle of Indian cult images. In Devendra Handa, ed., *Indological Studies: Essays in memory of Shri S.P. Singhal*. Delhi, Caxton Publications, 1987: 49-66.

959. **Srivastava, Rani**
Kusana kalin shilpakala me nritya. *Bulletin of Museums and Archaeoloy in U.P.*, No. 14, December 1974: 38-48. (Hindi).

960. _____.
Mathura kala ke do naye abhipraya. *Bulletin of Museums and Archaeology in U.P.*, Nos. 33-34, June-December 1984: 19-24. (Hindi)

961. **Srivastava, V.N.**
Gupta sculpture at Mathura. *Marg*, Vol. 15, No. 2, March 1962: 50-58.

962. **Srivstava, V.N.** and **Misra, Shivadhar**
Inventory of Mathura Museum sculptures since 1939 uptodate. *Bulletin of Museums and Archaeology in U.P.*, Nos. 11-12, June-December 1973: 42-122.

963. **Stacy, L.R.**
Note on the discovery of a relic of Grecian sculpture in Upper India. *Journal of the Asiatic Society of Bengal*, Vol. 5, 1836: 567-570.

964. **Sundaram, K.**
Monumental art and architecture of India. Bombay, D.B. Taraporevala Sons & Co., 1974.

965. **Talim, Meena**
Love of one's country in Mathura art. *Indica*, Vol. 21, No. 2, September 1984: 75-79.

966. **Tewari, S.P.**
Nupura: The anklet in Indian literature and art. Delhi, Agam Kala Prakashan, 1982.

967. **Tiwari, Girija Shankar**
Pracheen dhatu murtiyan. *Uttar Pradesh*, Vol. 9, No. 12, May 1981: 91-94, 104. (Hindi)

968. **Tomory, Edith**
A history of fine arts in India and the west. Bombay, Orient Longman, 1982.

969. _____.
Introduction to the history of fine arts in India and the west. Bombay, Orient Longman, 1968.

970. **Trivedi, S.D.**
Masterpieces of Mathura Museum. *Journal of Indian Museums*, Vol. 29, 1973: 30-32.

971. **Trubner, Henry**
The art of Greater India. *Oriental Art*, New Series, Vol. 3, No. 1, 1950: 33-39.

972. Uni tete sculpture de L'Ecole de Mathura. *Arts Asiatiques*, Vol. 4, No. 1, 1957: 71-75. (French)

973. **Upadhyaya, Bhagwat Sharan**
Bharatiya kala aur sanskriti ki bhumika. Delhi, Ranjit Printers and Publishers, 1965. (Hindi)

974. **Upadhyaya, B.S.**
Sculptures in the Provincial Museum, Lucknow. *Journal of the Indian Society of Oriental Art*, Vol. 10, 1942: 175-190.

975. **Upadhyaya, Padma**
Female images in the museums of Uttar Pradesh and their social background. Varanasi, Chaukhamba Orientalia, 1978.

976. **Veraardi, Giovanni,** With a note by **Alessandro Grossato.**
The Kusana Emperors as Cakravartins. Dynastic art and cults in India and Central Asia: History of a theory, clarifications and refutations. *East and West*, New Series, Vol. 33, 1983: 225-294.

977. **Vogel, J. Ph.**
Archaeological Museum at Mathura. Delhi, Indological Book House, 1971.

978. _____.
The Mathura School of sculpture. *Archaeological Survey of India Annual Report*, 1906-07: 137-160.

979. _____.
The Mathura School of sculpture. *Archaeological Survey of India Annual Report*, 1909-10: 63-79.

980. _____.
La sculputre de Mathura. *Ars Asiatica*, Vol. 15, 1930.

981. _____.
A statue of king Kanishka. *Journal of the Panjab Historical Society*, Vol. 2, No. 1: 39-49.

982. **Williams, Joanna G.**
The art of Gupta India; empire and province. New Delhi, Heritage Publishers, 1983.

983. _____.
The case of the omitted hundreds: Stylistic development in Mathura sculpture of the Kusana period. In Doris Meth Srinivasan, ed., *Mathura: The cultural heritage*. New Delhi, American Institute of Indian Studies, 1989: 325-331.

984. **Woodward, Hiram W., Jr.**
Such as awakening: Indian sculpture from the Museum of Fine Arts, Boston. Vermont, Robert Hull Fleming Museum, 1984.

985. **Zimmer, Heinrich**
The art of Indian Asia. New York, Bollingen Foundation, 1960. 2 Vols.

HINDU

986. **Agrawala, P.K.**
The early Indian Mother-goddess votive discs. *East and West*, New Series, Vol. 29, 1979: 75-111.

987. _____.
Goddess Vinayaki: The female Ganesa. Varanasi, Prithivi Prakashan, 1978.

988. _____.
Iconoplastic beginnings of multi-headed and multi-armed images at Mathura. *Journal of the Indian Society of Oriental Art*, New Series, Vol. 15, 1985-86: 21-28.

989. _____.
Identification of the so-called Nagi figures as goddess Sasthi. *East and West*, New Series, Vol. 21, Nos. 3-4, September-December 1971: 325-329.

990. _____.
Skanda-Karttikeya: A study in the origin and development. Varanasi, Banaras Hindu University, 1967.

991. _____.
Srivatsa: The babe of goddess Sri. Varanasi, Prithivi Prakashan, 1974.

992. **Agrawala, R.C.**
Four-faced Siva and four-faced Visnu at Mathura. *Vishveshvaranand Indological Journal*, Vol. 3, pt. 1, March 1965: 107-110.

993. _____.
Gandhara Skanda with flames. *East and West*, New Series, Vol. 18, Nos. 1-2, March-June 1968: 163-165.

994. _____.
The goddess Mahisasuramardini in early Indian art. *Artibus Asiae*, Vol. 21, 1958: 123-130.

995. _____.
Goddess Sasthi in Mathura sculptures. *Bulletin of Museums and Archaeology in U.P.*, No 4, December 1969: 1-6.

996. _____.
Krsna and Baladeva as attendant figures in early Indian sculpture. *Indian Historical Quarterly*, Vol. 38, No. 1, March 1962: 86-88.

997. _____.
Mathura-kala ki do aditiya prastar-pratimaen. *Maru-Bharati*, Vol. 9, No. 4, January 1962: 33-34. (Hindi)

998. _____.
Matrka reliefs in early Indian art. *East and West*, New Series, Vol. 21, Nos. 1-2, March-June 1971: 79-89.

999. _____.
Rajasthan ke pracheen shila-lekho va pratimaon me 'Ardha-narisvar' bhav ki abhivayakti. *Maru-Bharati*, Vol. 6, No. 2, July 1958: 43-44. (Hindi)

1000. _____.
Rajasthan ki pracheen murtikala me Sivalinga. *Maru-Bharati*, Vol. 19, No. 4, January 1972: 41-43. (Hindi)

1001. _____.
Rajasthan's contribution to early Brahmanic iconography. In *Investigating Indian art*. Berlin, Staatliche Museen Preussischer Kulturbesitz, 1987: 13-24.

1002. _____.
A sculpture of karttikeya. *The Adyar Library Bulletin*, Vol. 24, pts. 3-4, December 1960: 149-152.

1003. _____.
Videshi sangrahalayon me Mathura kala ki advitiya Mahisamardini pratimaen. *Bulletin of Museums and Archaeology in U.P.*, Nos. 41-42, June-December 1988: 57-58. (Hindi)

1004. **Agrawala, V.S.**
Brahmanical images in Mathura. *Journal of the Indian Society of Oriental Art*, Vol. 5, 1937: 122-130.

1005. _____.
A catalogue of the Brahmanical images in Mathura art. Lucknow, U.P. Historical Society, 1951.

1006. _____.
A catalogue of the images of Brahma, Vishnu and Siva in Mathura art. *Journal of the U.P. Historical Society*, Vol. 22, pts. 1-2, 1949: 102-210.

1007. _____.
An early Brahmanical relief from Mathura. *Journal of the U.P. Historical Society*, Vol. 10, pt. 2, December 1937: 30-34.

1008. _____.
Four new Yaksha statues. *Journal of the U.P. Historical Society*, Vols. 24-25, 1951-1952: 186-190.

1009. _____.
Mathura kala me Brahman dharma-sambandhi devataon ki murtiyan. *Hindustani*, Vol. 7, No. 1, January 1937: 1-16. (Hindi)

1010. _____.
A note on a Gupta Shiva linga at Mathura. *Journal of the U.P. Historical Society*, Vol. 8, pt. 1, July 1935: 83-85.

1011. _____.
A note on the God Naigamesha. *Journal of the U.P. Historical Society*, Vol. 20, 1947: 68-73.

1012. _____.
A note on the new Mathura head. *Journal of the U.P. Historical Society*, Vol. 12, pt. 2, December 1939: 107-108.

1013. _____.
A syrnix-player in Mathura art. *Journal of the U.P. Historical Society*, Vol. 17, pt. 2, December 1944: 71-72.

1014. **Bajpai, K.D.**
Mathura-kala me Brahma. In *Sampurnanand abhinandan granth*. Varanasi, Nagri Pracharini Sabha, 1950: 153-163. (Hindi)

1015. _____.
Mathura-kala me Krishna-Balaram ki murtiyan. *Kala-Nidhi*, Vol. 1, No. 2: 133-135. (Hindi).

1016. _____.
A new inscribed image of a Yaksha. In *India Antigua: A volume of oriental studies presented by his friends and pupils to Jean Philippe Vogel on the occasion of the fiftieth anniversary of his doctorate*. Leyden, E.J. Brill, 1947: 8-9.

1017. _____.
A new Kusana image of Indra in the Mathura Museum. *Proceedings and Transactions of All-India Oriental Conference*, Session 13, pt. 3, 1946: 80.

1018. _____.
A note on two ashtabhuji images of Vishnu from Mathura. *Indian History Congress, Proceedings*, Session 14, 1951: 78-79.

1019. _____.
Sri Krsna ka veer roop. *Bulletin of Museums and Archaeology in U.P.*, Nos. 21-14, June 1978-December 1979: 59-66. (Hindi)

1020. _____.
Sri Krishna: Sahitya aur puratattva me. In Thakur Prasad Verma and others, ed., *Yugayugina Vraja*. Varanasi, Bharatiya Itihasa Samkalan Samiti, U.P., 1988: 86-91. (Hindi)

1021. _____.
Two rare images of Vishnu from Mathura. *Journal of the U.P. Historical Society*, Vol. 2, pt. 2, New Series, 1954: 17-19.

1022. Balarama image, Bajna, district Mathura. *Indian Archaeology: A Review*, 1974-75: 71.

1023. **Bandyopadhyay, Samaresh**
Ardhanarisvara and a coin of Kaniska. In D.C. Sircar, ed., *Pracyavidya Tarangini: Golden Jubilee Volume of the Department of Ancient Indian History and Culture.* Calcutta, University of Calcutta, 1969: 218-221.

1024. **Banerjea, J.N.**
The development of Hindu iconography. Calcutta, University of Calcutta, 1956.

1025. _____.
Images of Samba. *Journal of the Indian Society of Oriental Art*, Vol. 12, 1944: 129-134.

1026. _____.
Surya, Adityas and Navagrahas. *Journal of the Indian Society of Oriental Art*, Vol. 16, 1948: 47-100.

1027. **Banerjee, P.**
The life of Krishna in Indian art. New Delhi, National Museum, 1978.

1028. **Bautze, J.**
A note on two Matrka panels. In *Investigating Indian art*. Berlin, Staatliche Museen Preussischer Kulturbesitz, 1987: 25-30.

1029. **Begley, W.E.**
Visnu's flaming wheel: The iconography of the Sudarsana-Cakra. New York, New York University Press, 1973.

1030. **Bhattacharyya, Haridas**
Sarasvati the goddess of learning. In *Commemorative essays presented to Professor Kashinath Bapuji Pathak*. Poona, Bhandarkar Oriental Research Institute, 1934: 32-52.

1031. **Butcher, G.M.**
The new Indian art galleries in the Victoria and Albert Museum, London. *Oriental Art*, New Series, Vol. 3, No. 1; 1957: 28-29.

1032. **Carter, Martha L.**
The Bacchants of Mathura: New evidence of Dionysiac Yaksha imagery from Kushan Mathura. *Bulletin of the Cleveland Museum of Art*, Vol. 69, No. 8, October 1982: 247-257.

1033. **Chakravarti, Mahadev**
The concept of Rudra-Siva through the ages. Delhi, Motilal Banarsidass, 1986.

1034. **Chanda, Ramaprasad**
The Brahmanic sculpture of the Gupta period. *Indian Museum Bulletin*, Vol. 14, 1979: 134-138.

1035. _____.
Four ancient Yaksa statues. *Indian Museum Bulletin*, Vol. 11, No. 1, January 1976: 7-21.

1036. **Coomaraswamy, A.K.**
Early Indian iconography: Indra, with special reference to "Indra's visit". *Eastern Art*, Vol. 1, No. 1, July 1928: 32-41.

1037. _____.
Early Indian iconography: Sri-Lakshmi. *Eastern Art*, Vol. 1, No. 3, January 1929: 175-189.

1038. _____.
Surya (The Sun-god). *Bulletin of the Museums of Fine Arts, Boston*, Vol. 20, No. 122, December 1922: 72-73.

1039. _____.
Yaksas. New Delhi, Munshiram Manhoralal, 1971. 2 Parts.

1040. **Darian, Steven**
The Ganges in Indian art. *East and West*, New Series, Vol. 23, Nos. 3-4, September-December 1973: 307-325.

1041. **Desai, Kalpana S.**
Iconography of Visnu. New Delhi, Abhinav Publications, 1973.

1042. **Dhavalikar, M.K.**
Ganesa in Mathura. In B.M. Pande and B.D. Chattopadhyaya, ed., *Archaeology and history: Essays in memory of Shri A. Ghosh*, Vol. 2. Delhi, Agam Kala Prakashan, 1987: 471-478.

1043. **Diskalkar, D.B.**
Antiquity of the image of Mahisasuramardini. *Indian Historical Quarterly*, Vol. 22, No. 1, March 1946: 154-155.

1044. _____.
Some Brahmanical sculptures in the Mathura Museum. *Journal of the U.P. Historical Society*, Vol. 5, pt. 1, January 1932: 18-57.

1045. **Gail, Adalbert J.**
On the symbolism of three- and four-faced Visnu images: A reconsideration of evidence. *Artibus Asiae*, Vol. 44, 1983: 297-307.

1046. **Ghosh, Niranjan**
Sri Sarasvati in Indian art and literature. Delhi, Sri Satguru Publications, 1984.

1047. **Giri, Kamal**
A note on a recently acquired Vamana image in the Bharat Kala Bhavan. *East and West*, New Series, Vol. 28, 1978: 253-256.

1048. **Jayaswal, Kusum**
Pracheen Saraswati pratimaen. *Uttar Pradesh*, Vol. 9, No. 12, May 1981: 58-61. (Hindi)

1049. **Jitendra Kumar**
Bharna kala ki Sunga kalin Yaksha aur Manasi Ganga ki madhyakalin praster-pratimaen: Mathura. *Dhayanam*, Vols. 5-6, 1985-86: 51-54. (Hindi)

1050. **Joshi, N.P.**
Brahmanical sculptures in the State Museum, Lucknow. Lucknow, State Museum, 1989, part 2, Vols. 1-2.

1051. _____.
Catalogue of the Brahmanical sculptures in the State Museum, Lucknow. Lucknow, The State Museum, 1972. Part 1.

1052. _____.
Devi Ekansha ki Kushan kalin murtiyan. *Bulletin of Museums and Archaeology in U.P.*, No. 1, March 1968: 24-29. (Hindi)

1053. _____.
Devi Sannamukhi ya Sasthi. *Bulletin of Museums and Archaeology in U.P.*, No. 3, June 1969: 38-41. (Hindi)

1054. _____.
Early Brahmanical sculptures in Bharat Kala Bhavan. In Anand Krishna and Chandramani Singh, ed., *Chhavi: Golden Jubilee Volume*. Varanasi, Bharat Kala Bhavan, 1971: 178-182.

1055. _____.
Early forms of Siva. In Michael W. Meister, ed., *Discourses on Siva: Proceedings of a symposium on the nature of religious imagery*. Bombay, Vakils, Feffer & Simons, 1984: 47-61.

1056. _____.
Ekanamsa in early Kusana art. *Journal of the Indian Society of Oriental Art*, New Series, Vol. 2, 1967-1968: 34-36.

1057. _____.
Iconography of Balarama. New Delhi, Abhinav Publications, 1979.

1058. _____.
Images of Visnu in the Kusana art from Mathura. *Bharati*, Nos. 12-14, 1968-1971: 21-43.

1059. _____.
Krsna in art—whether two-armed or multi-armed. *Bulletin of Museums and Archaeology in U.P.*, Nos. 21-24, June 1978-December 1979: 19-25.

1060. _____.
Kusana kala me Sri Krsna. *Sri Krsna-Sandesh*, Vol. 1, No. 1, 1965: 85-87. (Hindi)

1061. _____.
Kusana Varaha sculpture. *Arts Asiatiques*, Vol. 12, 1965: 113-117.

1062. _____.
Matrka figures in Kusana sculptures at Mathura. In *Investigating Indian art*. Berlin, Staatliche Museen Preussischer Kulturbesitz, 1987: 159-171.

1063. _____.
Matrkas mothers in Kusana art. New Delhi, Kanak Publications, 1986.

1064. _____.
On the iconography of Balarama in the north India. *Bulletin of Museums and Archaeology in U.P.*, No. 10, December 1972: 15-25.

1065. _____.
Prarambhik Vishnu Pratimayen. Varanasi, Bharatiya Vidya Prakashan, 1969. (Hindi)

1066. _____.
Prarambhik Visnu-murtiyon ka ek adhyayana. *Bulletin of Museums and Archaeology in U.P.*, No. 2, December 1968: 6-26. (Hindi)

1067. _____.
Some unnoticed finds of iconographic interest. *East and West*, New Series, Vol. 22, Nos. 1-2, March-June 1972: 41-49.

1068. _____.
Two Matrka plaques in the State Museum, Lucknow. *Bulletin of Museums and Archaeology in U.P.*, No. 1, March 1968: 18-23.

1069. **Kramrisch, Stella**
A Siva head from Mathura. *Journal of the Indian Society of Oriental Art*, Vol. 6, 1938: 200-202.

1070. **Kreisel, Gerd**
Die Siva-Bildwerke der Mathura-kunst. Stuttgart, Franz Steiner Verlag Wiesbaden GMBH, 1986. (German).

1071. **Krishna, Nanditha**
The art and iconography of Vishnu-Narayana. Bombay, D.B. Taraporevala Sons & Co., 1980.

1072. **Maxwell, T.S.**
The evidence for a Visvarupa iconographic tradition in western India, 6th-9th centuries A.D. *Artibus Asiae*, Vol. 44, 1983: 213-234.

1073. _____.
Vivsarupa. Delhi, Oxford University Press, 1988.

1074. Medieval sculptures; Adniga, district Mathura. *Indian Archaeology: A Review*, 1982-83: 139.

1075. **Misra, O.P.**
Iconography of the Saptamatrikas. Delhi, Agam Kala Prakashan, 1989.

1076. **Misra, R.N.**
Kubera and Mudgarapani on a Mathura railing pillar: An identification. *Bulletin of Museums and Archaeology in U.P.*, Nos. 5-6, June-December 1970: 28-30.

1077. _____.
Yaksha cult and iconography. New Delhi, Munshiram, Manoharlal, 1981.

1078. **Mitterwallner, Gritle V.**
Evolution of the Linga. In Michael W. Meister, ed., *Discourses on Siva: Proceedings of symposium on the nature of religious imagery*. Bombay, Vakils, Faffer & Simons, 1984: 12-31.

1079. _____.
The Kusana type of the goddess Mahisasuramardini as compared to the Gupta and mediaeval types. In *German Scholars on India*, Vol. 2, Bombay, Nachiketa Publications, 1976: 196-213.

1080. _____.
Yaksas of ancient Mathura. In Doris Meth Srinivasan, ed., *Mathura: The cultural heritage*. New Delhi, American Institute of Indian Studies, 1989: 368-382.

1081. **Nagar, M.M.**
A new image of Agni from Mathura. *Journal of the U.P. Historical Society*, Vol. 19, pts. 1-2, July-December 1946: 52-55.

1082. _____.
A new image of Rahu from Mathura. *Indian History Congress, Proceedings*, Session 3, 1939: 446-448.

1083. **Nagar, Shanti Lal**
Mahishasuramardini in Indian art. New Delhi, Aditya Prakashan, 1988.

1084. **Pal, Pratapaditya**
A Kushan Indra and some related sculptures. *Oriental Art*, New Series, Vol. 25, No. 2, 1979: 212-226.

1085. **Pandey, Sudhakar**
Ganga & Yamuna in Indian art & literature. Chandigarh, Indra Prakashan, 1984.

1086. **Preciado-Solis, Benjamin**
The Krsna cycle in the puranas: Themes and motifs in a heroic saga. Delhi, Motilal Banarsidass, 1984.

1087. **Ramachandran, K.S.** and **Krishnamurti, C.**
Hermaphroditism and early Ardhanarisvara figures in India. *Vishveshvaranand Indological Journal*, Vol. 2, pt. 1, March 1964: 123-125.

1088. **Ray, S.C.**
Evolution of Hindu-Buddhist art in the Gangetic Valley: A study on the basis of stratigraphic evidence of archaeological excavations. In *Investigating Indian art*. Berlin, Staatliche Museen Preussischer Kulturbesitz, 1987: 273-290.

1089. **Roy, Udai Narain**
Salabhanjika in art, philosophy and literature. Allahabad, Lokbharati Publications, 1979.

1090. **Sahai, Bhagwant**
Iconography of minor Hindu and Buddhist deities. New Delhi, Abhinav Publications, 1975.

1091. **Sahni, Daya Ram**
A Mathura image of the Naga Dadhikarnna of the Kushan period. *Archaeological Survey of India Annual Report*, 1924-25: 149-150.

1092. _____.
A stone sculpture representing an incident from the life of Krishna. *Archaeological Survey of India Annual Report*, 1925-26: 183-184.

1093. **Sarma, I.K.**
The development of early Saiva art and architecture. Delhi, Sundeep Prakashan, 1982.

1094. **Sengupta, R.**
A note on the fish attribute of Varahi. *Bulletin of Museums and Archaeology in U.P.*, No. 10, December 1972: 12.

1095. **Shah, U.P.**
Lakulisa: Saivite Saint. In Michael W. Meister, ed., *Discourses on Siva: Proceedings of a symposium on the nature of religious imagery*. Bombay, Vakils, Feffer & Simons, 1984: 92-102.

1096. **Sharma, B.N.**
Iconography of Sadasiva. New Delhi, Abhinav Publications, 1976.

1097. _____.
Iconography of Vainayaki. New Delhi, Abhinav Publications, 1979.

1098. _____.
An image of Haragauri from Mathura. *Journal of Indian Museums*, Vol. 29, 1973: 40-42.

1099. _____.
Kusana Siva-Lingas from Mathura. *Journal of the Oriental Institute*, Vol. 27, Nos. 1-2, September -December 1977: 33-39.

1100. _____.
A rare image of Gajalaksmi from Mathura in the National Museum, New Delhi. *Bulletin of Ancient Indian History and Archaeology,* No. 2, 1968: 73-75.

1101. _____.
Revanta in literature, art and epigraphs. *East and West*, New Series, Vol. 23, Nos. 1-2, March-June 1973: 155-168.

1102. _____.
Vainayiki in medieval Indian art. *Oriental Art*, New Series, Vol. 16, No. 2, 1970: 169-172.

1103. **Sharma, R.C.**
Two new rare sculptures in Mathura Museum. *Bulletin of Museums and Archaeology in U.P.*, No. 10, December 1972: 65-67.

1104. _____.
Two new rare sculptures in Mathura Museum. *Journal of the Indian Society of Oriental Art*, New Series, Vol. 5, 1972-1973: 50-52.

1105. **Singh, Sheo Bahadur**
Brahmanical icons in northern India. New Delhi, Sagar Publications, 1977.

1106. **Sivaramamurti, C.**
Satarudriya: Vibhuti of Siva's iconography. New Delhi, Abhinav Publications, 1976.

1107. _____.
Sri Lakshmi in Indian art and thought. New Delhi, Kanak Publications, 1982.

1108. _____.
The weapons of Vishnu. *Artibus Asiae*, Vol. 18, No. 2, 1955: 128-136.

1109. **Sri Bhagwan Singh**
Guptakalin Hindu deva-pratimayen. New Delhi, Ramanand Vidya Bhawan, 1982. (Hindi)

1110. **Srinivasan, Doris**
Early Krsna icons: The case at Mathura. *Bulletin of Museums and Archaeology in U.P.*, Nos. 21-24, June 1978-December 1979: 1-18.

1111. _____.
Early Krishna icons: The case at Mathura. In Joanna G. Williams, ed., *Kaladarsana: American Studies in the art of India*. New Delhi, American Institute of Indian Studies, 1981: 127-136.

1112. _____.
Early Vaisnava imagery: Caturvyuha and variant forms. *Archives of Asian Art*, Vol. 32, 1979: 39-54.

1113. _____.
God as Brahmanical ascetic: A colossal Kusana icon of the Mathura School. *Journal of the Indian Society of Oriental Art*, New Series, Vol. 10, 1978-1979: 1-16.

1114. _____.
Indological studies of recent Mathura acquisitions in the Bharat Kala Bhavan. In Anand Krishna and Kamal Giri, ed., *Chhavi - 2: Rai Krishnadasa felicitation volume.* Varanasi, Bharat Kala Bhavan, 1981: 98-104.

1115. **Srinivasan, Doris Meth**
Significance and scope of pre-Kusana Saivite iconography. In Michael W. Meister, ed., *Discourses on Siva: Proceedings of a symposium on the nature of religious imagery.* Bombay, Vakils, Feffer & Simons, 1984: 32-46.

1116. _____
A unique Mathura eight-armed Visnu of the 4th century A.D. *Oriental Art*, New Series, Vol. 34, No. 4, 1988/89: 276-281.

1117. _____.
Vaisnava art and iconography at Mathura. In Doris Meth Srinivasan, ed., *Mathura: The cultural heritage*. New Delhi, American Institute of Indian Studies, 1989: 383-392.

1118. **Srivastava, A.K.**
Siva-Linga with Ganas, a new find from Mathura. *Artibus Asiae*, Vol. 43, No. 3, 1981-1982: 236-238.

1119. **Srivastava, Rani**
Mathura kala me Linga puja. *Uttar Pradesh*, Vol. 16, No. 9, February 1988: 13-15. (Hindi)

1120. **Srivastava, V.C.**
Surya in Mathura art. In Thakur Prasad Verma and others, ed., *Yugayugina Vraja*. Varanasi, Bharatiya Itihasa Samkalan Samiti, U.P., 1988: 78-85.

1121. **Stadtner, Donald M**
The tradition of Krsna pillars in North India. *Archives of Asian Art*, Vol. 40, 1987: 56-68.

1122. **Stern, Philippe**
A Nagaraja from Mathura. *Journal of the Indian Society of Oriental Art*, Vol. 3, No. 1, June 1935: 33-35.

1123. **Tewari, S.P.**
Identification of a Naga panel delineated on a door lintel from Sonkh. In Lokesh Chandra and others, ed., *Dimensions of Indian art: Pupul Jayakar seventy*, Vol. 1. Delhi, Agam Kala Prakashan, 1986: 523-532.

1124. **Thakur, Upendra**
Karttikeya in literature, art and coins. *East and West*, New Series, Vol. 24, Nos. 3-4, September-December 1974: 297-310.

1125. _____.
On Karttikeya. Varanasi, Chaukhambha Orientalia, 1981.

1126. **Trivedi, R.D.**
Visnu and his incarnations in the works of Kalidasa. *East and West*, New Series, Vol. 22, Nos. 1-2, March-June 1972: 51-62.

1127. **Trivedi, S.D.**
Fresh light on some icons of Mathura Museum. In A.M. Shastri and others, ed., *Vajapeya: Essays on evolution of Indian art & culture: Prof. K.D. Bajpai felicitation volume*, Vol. 2. Delhi, Agam Kala Prakashan, 1987: 211-215.

1128. **Upadhyaya, Shyamanand**
Rajya Sangrahalaya, Lucknow me sangrahit matrka patta. *Bulletin of Museums and Archaeology in U.P.*, Nos. 27-28, June-December 1981: 69-81. (Hindi)

1129. **Viennot, Odette**
The goddess Mahishasuramardini in Kushana art. *Artibus Asiae*, Vol. 19, 1956: 368-373.

1130. **Vijay Krishna**
Prasadhika or 'Sri'. *Journal of the Indian Society of Oriental Art*, New Series, Vol. 14, 1984-85: 59-67.

1131. Yakshi or devata under an Ashoka tree, Cleveland Museum of Art, Cleveland. *Archives of Asian Art*, Vol. 20, 1966-1967: 87.

BUDDHIST

1132. **Agrawala, V.S.**
Dhyani Buddhas and Bodhisattvas. *Journal of the U.P. Historical Society*, Vol. 11, pt. 2, December 1938: 1-13.

1133. ———.
Mathura ki Baudha kala. *Nagari Pracharani Patrika*, Vol. 13, No. 1, 1932: 17-46. (Hindi)

1134. ———.
A new Bodhisattva and a Bacchanalian group from Mathura. *Journal of the Indian Society of Oriental Art*, Vol. 6, 1938: 68-72.

1135. ———.
A new inscribed image of Kasyapa Buddha from Mathura. *Journal of the U.P. Historical Society*, Vol. 10, pt. 2, December 1937: 35-38.

1136. ———.
Vasudhara. *Journal of the Indian Society of Oriental Art*, Vol. 7, 1939: 13-17.

1137. **Anand, Mulk Raj**
Origin of the Buddha image. *Marg*. Vol. 15, No. 2, March 1962: 8-14.

1138. **Bajpai, K.D.**
Mathura Sangrahalaya ki navin Tara murti. *Shiksha*, July 1950: 96. (Hindi)

1139. _____.
New Buddhist finds from Mathura. *Lalit Kala*, Nos. 3-4: 102-104.

1140. **Banerjea, J.N.**
Usnisa-siraskata (a mahapurusa laksana) in the early Buddha images of India. *Indian Historical Quarterly*, Vol. 7, No. 3, September 1931: 499-514.

1141. Buddha Jayanti exhibition: Catalogue of exhibition of Buddhist art. Calcutta, Indian Museum, 1956.

1142. **Chanda, Ramaprasad**
The hair and the usnisa on the head of the Buddhas and the Jinas. *Indian Historical Quarterly*, Vol. 7, No. 3, September 1931: 669-673.

1143. _____.
The hair and the usnisa on the head of the Buddhas and the Jinas. *Indian Museum Bulletin*, Vol. 14, 1979: 132-134.

1144. **Codrington, K. de B.**
Mathura of the Gods. *Marg*, Vol. 9, No. 2: 41-49.

1145. **Coomaraswamy, A.K.**
The Buddha's cuda, hair, usnisa, and crown. *Journal of the Royal Asiatic Society of Great Britain and Ireland*, 1928: 815-841.

1146. _____.
Buddhist sculpture. *Museum of Fine Arts Bulletin, Boston*, Vol. 20, No. 120, August 1922: 45-53.

1147. _____.
Indian stone sculpture. *Museum of Fine Arts Bulletin, Boston*. Vol. 17, No. 104, December 1919: 57-63.

1148. _____.
The origin of the Buddha image. New Delhi, Munshiram Manoharlal, 1972.

1149. _____.
Some early Buddhist reliefs identified. *Journal of the Royal Asiatic Society of Great Britain and Ireland*, 1928: 390-398.

1150. **Czuma, Stanislaw**
A Gupta style bronze Buddha. *Bulletin of the Cleveland Museum of Art*, Vol. 57, No. 2, February 1970: 55-67.

1151. **Daridan, Jean**
Remarks on Mathuran Buddhist sculpture. In Anand Krishna and Chandramani Singh, ed., *Chhavi: Golden Jubilee Volume*. Varanasi, Bharat Kala Bhavan, 1971: 37-42.

1152. **Dehejia, Vidya**
Stupas and sculptures of early Buddhism. *Asian Art*, Vol. 2, No. 3, 1989: 7-31.

1153. Exhibition of Buddhist art and antiquities. Rangoon, Ministry of Union Culture, 1955.

1154. **Foucher, A.**
The beginnings of Buddhist art and other essays in Indian and Central-Asian archaeology. Paris, Paul Geuthner, 1917.

1155. _____.
On the iconography of the Buddha's nativity. Delhi, Manager of Publications, 1934. (Memoirs of the Archaeological Survey of India, No. 46).

1156. **Gaur, R.C.**
A rare Buddha image. *Journal of the Indian Society of Oriental Art*, Vol. 2, 1967-1968: 66-68.

1157. **Grunwedel, Albert**
Buddhist art in India. Spain, Susil Gupta, 1965.

1158. **Haesner, Chh.**
Some common stylistic and iconographic features in the Buddhist art of India and Central Asia. In *Investigating Indian art*. Berlin, Staatliche Museen Preussischer Kulturbesitz, 1987: 105-120.

1159. **Hallade, Madeleine**
The Gandhara style and the evolution of Buddhist art. London, Thames and Hudson, 1968.

1160. **Ingholt, Harald**
Gandhara art in Pakistan. New York, Pantheon Books, 1957.

1161. **Krishan, Y.**
The emergence of the Buddha image, Gandhara Versus Mathura. *Oriental Art*, New Series, Vol. 34, No. 4, 1988/89: 255-275.

1162. _____.
The hair on the Buddha's head and usnisa. *East and West*, New Series, Vol. 16, Nos. 3-4, September-December 1966: 275-289.

1163. _____.
The origin of the Buddha image. *Marg*, Vol. 15, No. 2, March 1962: 15-16.

1164. **Lalit Kumar**
A unique Bodhisattva head from Mathura. *Sambodhi*, Vol. 11, 1982-1983: 176-179.

1165. **Law, B.C.**
Sravasti in Indian literature. Delhi, Manager of Publications, 1935. (Memoirs of the Archaeological Survey of India, No. 50).

1166. **Malandra, Geri Hockfield**
Mara's army: Text and image in early Indian art. *East and West*, New Series, Vol. 31, 1981: 121-130.

1167. **Mallmann, Marie-Therese De**
Head-dresses with figurines in Buddhist art. *Indian Art and Letter*, New Series, Vol. 21, No. 2, 1947: 80-89.

1168. **Matics, Kathleen**
Thoughts pertaining to the "Maitreya" image in the Metropolitan Museum. *East and West*, New Series, Vol. 29, 1979: 113-126.

1169. **Misra, Shivadhar**
Mathura kala me jatak kathaen. In Radhey Shyam Dwivedi, ed., *Braj Vaibhav*, Mathura, Bharati Anusandhan Bhawan, 1972: 191-198. (Hindi)

1170. Muttra Museum. *Archaeological Survey of India Annual Report*, 1919-20: 41.

1171. **Myer, Prudence R.**
Bodhisattvas and Buddhas: Early Buddhist images from Mathura. *Artibus Asiae*, Vol. 42, No. 2, 1986: 107-142.

1172. **Narain, A.K.**
Unique inscribed Buddha image of the Mathura School of sculpture. *Journal of the Bihar Research Society*, Vol. 36, pts. 1-2, March & June 1950: 51-56.

1173. **Pal, Pratapaditya**
A pre-Kushan Buddha image from Mathura. *Marg*, Vol. 39, No. 4: 1-20.

1174. _____.
A pre-Kushan Buddha image from Mathura. In Pratapaditya Pal, ed., *A pot-pourri of Indian art*. Bombay, Marg Publications, 1988: 1-20.

1175. **Parimoo, Ratan**
Life of Buddha in Indian sculpture. New Delhi, Kanak Publications, 1982.

1176. **Patterson, Joby**
A mediaeval bronze from Swat and its connections with Kashmir. *Art and Archaeological Research Papers*, No. 13, June 1978: 50-54.

1177. **Paul, Debjani**
A Mathura medallion in the Patna Museum. *Oriental Art*, New Series, Vol. 25, No. 2, 1979: 231-239.

1178. **Ray, Nihar Ranjan**
Buddhist art and architecture in India after 250 A.D. *Roopa-Lekha*, Vol. 27, No. 1, 1956: 13-18.

1179. **Rhie, Marylin M.**
Some aspects of the relation of 5th century Chinese Buddha images with sculpture from N. India, Pakistan, Afghanistan and Central Asia. *East and West*, New Series, Vol. 26, Nos. 3-4, September-December 1976: 439-461.

1180. **Sabhapati Singh**
Baudha murtikala. *Kala-Saurabh*, Vol. 3, January 1974: 36-38. (Hindi)

1181. _____.
Baudha murtikala. *Kala-Saurabh*, Vol. 4, December 1975: 4-7. (Hindi)

1182. **Saunders, E. Dale**
Symbolic gestures in Buddhism. *Artibus Asiae*, Vol. 21, 1958: 47-63.

1183. **Sharma, R.C.**
Buddha as appears in Mathura art. *Journal of Indian Museums*, Vol. 29, 1973: 18-21.

1184. _____.
Buddhist art of Mathura. Delhi, Agam Kala Prakashan, 1984.

1185. _____.
Early phase of Buddhist icons at Mathura. *Bulletin of Museums and Archaeology in U.P.*, Nos. 33-34, June-December 1984: 57-66.

1186. _____.
Mathura kala me Buddha murti. In Radhey Shyam Dwivedi, ed., *Braj Vaibhav*. Mathura, Bharati Anusandhan Bhawan, 1972: 183-190. (Hindi).

1187. _____.
New Buddhist sculptures from Mathura (pre-Gupta epoch). *Bulletin of Museums and Archaeology in U.P.*, Nos. 17-18, June-December 1976: 1-10.

1188. _____.
New Buddhist sculptures from Mathura; pre Gupta epoch. *Lalit kala*, No. 19: 19-26.

1189. _____.
Pre-Kaniska Buddhist iconography at Mathura. *Bulletin of Museums and Archaeology in U.P.*, Nos. 5-6, June-December 1970: 16-27.

1190. _____.
Pre-Kanishka Buddhist iconography at Mathura. In Shataram Bhalchandra Deo, *Archaeological Congress and seminar papers: Papers presented at the 4th Annual Congress of the Indian Archaeological Society and the seminars held at Nagpur, 1970*. Nagpur, Nagpur University, 1972: 289-296.

1191. **Sivaramamurti, C.**
Catalogue 2500th Buddha Jayanti celebration 1956: Exhibition of Buddhist art. New Delhi, Lalit Kala Akademi, 1956.

1192. **Snellgrove. David L.**, ed.
The image of the Buddha. Paris, UNESCO, 1978.

1193. **Srinivasan, Doris Meth**
Depiction of the Buddha's genealogy in a Kusana relief and related sculpture. *Indian Museum Bulletin*, Vol. 21, 1986: 62-65.

1194. **Srivastava, A.L.**
Bharatiya kala me Buddha-janm. *Journal of the Ganganatha Jha Kendriya Sanskrita Bidyapeetha*, Vols. 38-39, 1982-1983: 9-17. (Hindi)

1195. **Srivastava, Virendra Nath**
Mathura ki navin abhilikhita Buddha murti, Saka Samvat 93 = 171-72 A.D. *Bulletin of Museums and Archaeological in U.P.*, No. 4, December 1969: 19-22. (Hindi).

1196. **Subramonia Iyer, S.**
Depiction of Buddha in the Kushana period. In A.M. Shastri and others, ed., *Vajapeya: Essays on evolution of Indian art & culture; Prof. K.D. Bajpai felicitation volume*, Vol. 2. Delhi, Agam Kala Prakashan, 1987: 283-284.

1197. **Tiwari, Pushpa**
Pracheen Buddha murtiyan: Ek tulnatamak adhyayan. In Krishna Deva and others, ed., *History and art*. Delhi, Raman-and Vidya Bhawan, 1989. (Hindi)

1198. **Trivedi, Vijay** and **Pandeya, Ram Naresh**
Krisna ki nagari ke garbh se jhankate Baudha itihas ke prastha. *Uttar Pradesh*, Vol. 7, No. 7, December 1978: 10-14. (Hindi)

1199. **Vogel, J.Ph.**
Buddhist art in India, Ceylon and Java. New Delhi, Oriental Books Reprint Corporation, 1977.

1200. _____.
De Buddhistische kunst van voor-Indie. Amsterdam. H.J. Paris, 1932. (Dutch)

1201. The way of the Buddha. New Delhi, Publications Division, 1956.

1202. **Williams, Joanna**
A Mathura Gupta Buddha reconsidered. *Lalit Kala*, No. 17: 28-32.

1203. _____.
Sarnath Gupta steles of the Budha's life. *Ars Oreintalis*, Vol. 10; 1975: 171-192.

1204. **Zwalf, W.**, ed.
Buddhism: Art and faith. London, British Museum Publications, 1985.

JAINA

1205. **Agrawala, Prem Kumar**
Jaina murtiyon ka kramik vikas. *Shraman*, Vol. 23, No. 4, February 1972: 18-21. (Hindi)

1206. **Agrawala, V.S.**
A fragmentary sculpture of Neminatha in the Lucknow Museum. *Jaina Antiquary*, Vol. 8, No. 2, December 1942: 45-49.

1207. _____.
Jaina art of Mathura. In *Chotte Lal Jain Smriti granth*. Calcutta, Babu Chotte Lal Jain Abhinandan Samiti, 1967: 87-91.

1208. _____.
Jaina Tirthankaras and other miscellaneous figures. Varanasi, Prithivi Prakashan, 1963.

1209. _____.
The nativity scene on a Jaina relief from Mathura. *Jaina Antiquary*, Vol. 10, No. 1, June 1944: 1-4.

1210. _____.
The presiding deity of child birth amongst the ancient Jainas with special reference to figures in the Mathura Museum. *Jaina Antiquary*, Vol. 2, No. 4, March 1937: 75-79.

1211. **Bajpai, K.D.**
Jain murtikala ka udbhav aur vikas. In Neelkantha Purushottam Joshi, ed., *Jain-nibandh-mala,* Vol. 1. Rampur, Babu Anand Kumar Jain Sansthan, 1977: 57-58. (Hindi)

1212. _____.
Mathura ke Jain vedika-stambh. *Jaina Siddhanta Bhaskar*, Vol. 20, No. 1, June 1953: 44-47. (Hindi)

1213. _____.
Mathura ki Jain kala. In *Srimad Rajendra Suri smarak granth.* Aahor, Sri Sandharmabrihatpagachchiya Jain Svetambar Sri Sangh, 1957: 608-11. (Hindi)

1214. _____.
Mathura se prapta Ambica ki ek naveen murti. *Jain Siddhanta Bhaskar*, Vol. 15, No. 2, January 1949: 132. (Hindi)

1215. _____.
New Jain images in the Mathura Museum. *Jaina Antiquary*, Vol. 13, No. 2, January 1948: 10-11.

1216. _____.
Tirthankara Muni-Suvrata in an inscribed Mathura sculpture in the Lucknow Museum. *Journal of the U.P. Historical Society*, Vols. 24-25, 1951-1952: 219-220.

1217. **Buhler, G.**
Jaina sculptures from Mathura. *Transactions of the International Congress of Orientalists*, 9, 1892: 219-221.

1218. **Chanda, Ramaprasad**
The Svetambara and the Digambara images of the Jinas. *Archaeological Survey of India Annual Report*, 1925-26: 176-182.

1219. ____.
The Svetambara and the Digambara images of the Jinas. *Indian Museum Bulletin*, Vol. 14, 1979: 128-132.

1220. **Fuhrer, A.**
Decorative ornaments from an ancient Jaina stupa at Mathura. *Technical Art Series,* 1894: Plates 8-9.

1221. **Harihar Singh**
Tirthankar-pratimaon ka udbhav aur vikas. *Shraman*, Vol. 25, Nos. 1-2, November-December 1973: 43-52. (Hindi)

1222. **Jain, Jyoti Prasad**
Mathura ki Jain kala. *Jain-Sandesh*, Vol. 20, 1964: 338-340. (Hindi)

1223. **Jain, Ramesh**
Jain murtikala me vedic dev pratiko ka lokik roopantar. *Rajasthan Bharati*, Vol. 15, No. 2, March 1973: 37-42. (Hindi)

1224. **Jain, Ramesh Chand**
Mathura ki Jaina kala. *Anekant*, Vol. 32, Nos. 1-2, January-June 1979: 26-29. (Hindi)

1225. **Jain, Sudha**
Jaina shilpakala aur Mathura. *Shraman*, Vol. 23, No. 12, October 1972: 16-19. (Hindi)

1226. **Joshi, M.C.**
North India. In A. Ghosh, ed., *Jaina art and architecture*, Vol. 2. New Delhi, Bharatiya Jnanpith, 1975: 239-260.

1227. **Joshi, N.P.**
Early Jaina icons from Mathura. In Doris Meth Srinivasan, ed., *Mathura: The cultural heritage*. New Delhi, American Institute of Indian Studies, 1989: 332-367.

1228. ____.
Mathura. In A. Ghosh, ed., *Jaina art and architecture*, Vol. 1. New Delhi, Bharatiya Jnanpith, 1974: 107-116.

1229. **Mitra, Debala**
Mathura. In A. Ghosh, ed., *Jaina art and architecture*, Vol. 1. New Delhi, Bharatiya Jnanpith, 1974: 49-68.

1230. **Mukhopadhyay, Mihir Mohan**
Mathura—the centre of Jaina art. In *Chotte Lal Jain Smriti granth*. Calcutta, Babu Chotte Lal Jain Abhinandan Samiti, 1967: 51-55.

1231. **Nagar, Madan Mohan**
Mathura ka Jaina stupa aur murtiyan. In *Premi abhinandana grantha*. Tikamgarh, Premi Abhinandana Grantha Samiti, 1946: 279-284. (Hindi)

1232. **Namdev, Shiv Kumar**
Bharatiya puratattva tatha me Bhagwan Mahavira. *Shraman*, Vol. 26 , Nos. 1-2, November-December 1974: 38-46. (Hindi)

1233. **Nigam, M.L.**
Impact of Jainism on Mathura art. *Journal of the U.P. Historical Society*, New Series, Vol. 9, pt. 1, 1961: 7-12.

1234. **Ramesh Chandra**
Mathura ki Jain kala. In Neelkantha Purushottam Joshi, ed., *Jain-nibandh-mala,* Vol. 1. Rampur, Babu Anand Kumar Jain Sansthan, 1977: 29-32. (Hindi)

1235. **Sengupta, R.**
The Jaina Ayaga-platforms at Mathura: An interpretation. *Bulletin of Museums and Archaeology in U.P.*, No. 9, June 1972: 23-29.

1236. **Shah, U.P.**
Beginnings of Jaina iconography. *Bulletin of Museums and Archaeological in U.P.*, No. 9, June 1972: 1-14.

1237. _____.
Iconography. In A. Ghosh, ed., *Jaina art and architecture*, Vol. 3. New Delhi, Bharatiya Jnanpith, 1975: 465-493.

1238. _____.
Jaina-rupa-mandana. New Delhi, Abhinav Publications, 1987.

1239. _____.
Studies in Jaina art. Banaras, Jaina Cultural Research Society, 1955.

1240. **Sharma, B.N.**
Jaina pratimayen. Delhi, Indological Book Corporation, 1979. (Hindi)

1241. _____.
Museums abroad: British Museum, London. In A. Ghosh, ed., *Jaina art and architecture*, Vol. 3. New Delhi, Bharatiya Jannpith, 1975: 537-544.

1242. **Sharma, R.C.**
The early phase of Jaina iconography. In *Chotte Lal Jain Smriti granth.* Calcutta, Babu Chotte Lal Jain Abhinandan Samiti, 1967: 57-61.

1243. _____.
Jaina sculptures of the Gupta age in the State Museum, Lucknow. In *Shri Mahavir Jaina Vidyalaya Golden Jubilee Volume*, pt. 1. Bombay, Shri Mahavira Jaina Vidyalaya, 1968: 143-155.

1244. _____.
Mathura sangrahalaya ki Kusana kaleen Jaina murtiyan. In Jyoti Prasad Jain, ed., *Bhagwan Mahavira Smriti granth.* Lucknow, Shri Mahavira Nirvana Samiti, 1975: 119-125. (Hindi)

1245. _____.
Mathura sangrahalaya ki Kusana kalin Jain murtiyan. In Neelkantha Purushottam Joshi, ed., *Jain-nibandh-mala*, Vol. 1. Rampur, Babu Anand Kumar Jain Sansthan, 1977: 17-25. (Hindi)

1246. **Shashi Kant**
Some unique Jain images. *East and West*, New Series, Vol. 26, Nos. 3-4, 1976: 435-438.

1247. **Sisodia, Vishnu**
A Jain goddess from Rajasthan. *East and West*, New Series, Vol. 19, Nos. 3-4, September-December 1969: 410-412.

1248. **Smith, Vincent, A.**
The Jaina stupa and other antiquities of Mathura. Allahabad, Goverment Press, 1901.

1249. **Srivastava, Virendra Nath**
Rajya Samgrahalaya ka neelanjana-patta. In Jyoti Prasad Jain., ed., *Bhagwan Mahavira Smriti granth.* Lucknow, Shri Mahavira Nirvana Samiti, 1975: 118. (Hindi)

1250. **Srivastava, V.N.**
Some interesting Jaina sculptures in the State Museum, Lucknow. *Bulletin of Museums and Archaeology in U.P.*, No. 9, June 1972: 45-52.

1251. **Tiwari, M.N.P.**
Ambika in Jaina art and literature. New Delhi, Bharatiya Jnanpith, 1989.

1252. _____.
Jain pratima-vijnana. Varanasi, Parsvanath Vidyashram Shodh-Sansthan, 1981. (Hindi)

1253. _____.
Mathura me Jain dharm aur kala. *Uttar Pradesh*, Vol. 10, No. 7, December 1981: 28-31. (Hindi)

1254. _____.
A note on some Bahubali images from North India. *East and West*, New Series, Vol. 23, Nos. 3-4, September-December 1973: 347-353.

1255. _____.
Uttar Bharatiya shilpa me Tirthankar Mahavira. *Shraman*, Vol. 21, No. 12, October 1970: 18-23. (Hindi)

1256. **Trivedi, Shiv Dayal**
Mathura sangrahalaya me Rsabhanath ki pratimaen. In Neelkantha Purushottam Joshi, ed., *Jain-nibandh-mala*, Vol. 1. Rampur, Babu Anand Kumar Jain Sansthan, 1977: 26-28. (Hindi)

1257. **Williams, Joanna**
Two new Gupta Jina images. *Oriental Art*, New Series, Vol. 18, No. 4, 1972: 378-380.

TERRACOTTAS

1258. **Agrawala, V.S.**
Mathura terracottas. *Journal of the U.P. Historical Society*, Vol. 9, pt. 2, July 1936: 6-38.

1259. _____.
Mathura terracottas. Varanasi, Prithivi Prakashan, 1984.

1260. _____.
A palace scene on a terracotta panel from Mathura. *Journal of the Indian Society of Oriental Art*, Vol. 10, 1942: 69-73.

1261. _____.
Some terracottas in the Baroda Museum. *Bulletin, Museum and Picture Gallery Baroda*, Vol. 12, 1955-56: 1-10.

1262. **Bajpai, K.D.**
A stone head and some new terracottas from Mathura. *Journal of Indian Museums*, Vol. 11, 1955: 34-36.

1263. **Banerji, Arundhati**
Terracotta art expression in Indian sub-continent. *Roopa-Lekha*, Vol. 56, 1984: 18-36.

1264. **Barrett, Douglas**
A terracotta plaque of Mahisasuramardini. *Oriental Art*, New Series, Vol. 21, No. 1; 1975: 64-67.

1265. **Billorey, Ramesh Kumar**
Social life as reflected in Maurya and Sunga terracottas. In D.C. Sircar, ed., *Social life in ancient India*. Calcutta, University of Calcutta, 1971: 143-147.

1266. **Dasgupta, Charu Chandra**
Some terracottas from Mathura preserved in the Francis Hopp Museum of Asiatic Arts. *Journal of the Royal Asiatic Society of Bengal, Letters*, Vol. 9, 1943: 211-220.

1267. **Dasgupta, C.C.**
Unpublished ancient Indian terracottas preserved in the Musee Guimet, Paris. *Artibus Asiae*, Vol. 14, 1951: 283-305.

1268. **Desai, Devangana**
Terracottas and urban culture of Ancient India (circa 600 B.C. - A.D. 600). *National Museum Bulletin*, Nos. 4-6: 59-65.

1269. **Dhavalikar, M.K.**
Masterpieces of Indian terracottas. Bombay, D.B. Taraporevala Sons & Co., 1977.

1270. **Gordon, D.H.**
Early Indian terracottas. *Journal of Indian Society of Oriental Art*, Vol. 11, 1943: 136-195.

1271. **Gupta, P.L.**
Gangetic valley terracotta art. Varanasi, Prithivi Prakashan, 1972.

1272. **Joshi, M.C.** and **Margabandhu, C.**
Some terracottas from excavations at Mathura — A study. *Journal of the Indian Society of Oriental Art*, New Series, Vol. 8, 1976-1977: 16-32.

1273. **Joshi, N.P.**
A new terracotta female figure from Mathura. *Journal of the U.P. Historical Society*, New Series, Vols. 11-13, pt. 2, 1965: 23-25.

1274. **Kala, S.C.**
Terracottas in the Allahabad Museum. New Delhi, Abhinav Publications, 1980.

1275. **Kramrisch, Stella**
Indian Terracottas. *Journal of the Indian Society of Oriental Art*, Vol. 7, 1939: 89-110.

1276. **Moti Chandra**
Terracottas in Bharat Kala Bhavan. In Anand Krishna and Chandramani Singh, ed., *Chhavi: Golden Jubilee Volume*. Varanasi, Bharat Kala Bhavan, 1971: 1-15.

1277. **Nagar, M.M.**
Some new terracottas from Mathura. *Journal of the U.P. Historical Society*, Vol. 17, pt. 2, December 1944: 73-75.

1278. **Pal, Pratapaditya**
Icons of piety images of whimsy: Asian terracottas from the Walter-Grounds collection. Los Angeles, Los Angeles County Museum of Art, 1987.

1279. **Poster, Amy G.**
From India earth: 4,000 years of terracotta art. New York, The Brooklyn Museum, 1986.

1280. **Prakash, Pratibha**
Terracotta animal figurines in the Ganga-Yamuna valley (600 B.C. to 600 A.D.). Delhi, Agam Kala Prakashan, 1985.

1281. **Sawoo, Mangala**
Some interesting Mathura terracotta figurines in the Indian Museum. *Indian Museum Bulletin*, Vol. 14, 1979: 91-94.

1282. **Shah, U.P.**
A Sunga terracotta from Mathura. *Bulletin of the Baroda Museum and Picture Gallery*, Vol. 7, pts. 1-2, 1949-1950: 17-19.

1283. **Sharma, R.C.**
Archaic terracotta divinities—a case study of Mathura. *Indian Museum Bulletin*, Vol. 21, 1986: 34-37.

1284. **Shukla, K.S.**
A unique terracotta Kusana royal figure. *Bulletin of Museums and Archaeology in U.P.*, Nos. 35-36, 1985: 11-13.

1285. **Srivastava, S.K.**
Identification of a terracotta plaque from Mathura. *Bharati*, No. 8, pt. 1, 1964-65: 92-94.

ARCHITECTURE

1286. **Cole, Henry Hardy**
Illustrations of buildings near Muttra and Agra showing the mixed Hindu-Mohamedan style of upper India. London, India Office, 1873.

1287. **Fergusson, James**
History of Indian and Eastern architecture. London, John Murray, 1910. 2 Vols.

1288. **Pathak, Visnu Chandra**
Braj ke vaibhavashali Durg. In Radhey Shyam Dwivedi, ed., *Braj Vaibhav*. Mathura, Bharati Anusandhan Bhawan, 1972: 163-167. (Hindi)

1289. **Prahlad Singh**
Stone observatories in India erected by Maharaja Sawai Jai Singh of Jaipur (1686-1743 A.D.) at Delhi, Jaipur, Ujjain, Varanasi, Mathura. Varanasi, Bharata Manisha, 1978.

1290. **Shah, U.P.**
A note on stone umbrellas from Mathura. *Journal of the U.P. Historical Society*, Vols. 24-25, 1951-1952: 205-208.

1291. **Singh, Ambika Prasad**
Mathura—Vrandavan ke kuchh mahatavapurna ghat evam mandir. In Thakur Prasad Verma and others, ed., *Yugayugina Vraja*. Varanasi, Bharatiya Itihasa Samkalan Samiti, U.P. 1988: 39-44. (Hindi)

1292. **Srivastava, V.N.**
Braj ki vastu kala. In Radhey Shyam Dwivedi, ed., *Braj Vaibhav*. Mathura, Bharati Anusandhan Bhawan, 1972: 173-178. (Hindi)

HINDU

1293. **Agrawala, P.K.**
Gupta temple architecture. Varanasi, Prithivi Prakashan, 1981.

1294. **Brown, Percy**
Indian architecture: Buddhist and Hindu periods. Bombay, D.B. Taraporevala Sons & Co., 1965.

1295. **Dixit, Uma Shankar**
Braj ke chaar pracheen dev-mandir. In Radhey Shyam Dwivedi, ed., *Braj Vaibhav*. Mathura, Bharati Anusandhan Bhawan, 1972: 241-245. (Hindi)

1296. _____.
Sri Dwarikadhisha mandir Mathura. In Radhey Shyam Dwivedi, ed., *Braj Vaibhav*. Mathura, Bharati Anusandhan Bhawan, 1972: 246-248. (Hindi)

1297. _____.
Vrindavan ke do sundar mandir. In Radhey Shyam Dwivedi, ed., *Braj Vaibhav*. Mathura, Bharati Anusandhan Bhawan, 1972: 269-275. (Hindi)

1298. **Dwivedi, Radhey Shyam**
Tirthmaya Mathura ke ghat. In Radhey Shyam Dwivedi, ed., *Braj Vaibhav*. Mathura, Bharati Anusandhan Bhawan, 1972: 252-254. (Hindi)

1299. **Hartel, Herbert**
A Kusana Naga temple at Sonkh. *Bulletin of Museums and Archaeology in U.P.*, Nos. 11-12, June-December 1973: 1-6.

1300. **Jain, Shobha Lal**
Vrindavan ka ek anutha mandir. *Uttar Pradesh*, Vol. 10, No. 11, April 1982: 15-17. (Hindi)

1301. **Krishna Deva**
Pan-Indian style; North India, c-250 B.C. A.D. 400: Mauryas, Sungas, Kanvas, Kusanas, Ksatrapas. In Michael W. Meister and others, ed., *Encyclopaedia of Indian temple architecture: North India; Foundations of North Indian style, c. 250 B.C.- A.D. 1100*, Vol. 2, part 1: Text and plates. New Delhi, American Institute of Indian Studies, 1988: 3-17.

1302. **Sharma, Devdhar**
Sri Bhagwadgita mandir Mathura. In Radhey Shyam Dwivedi, ed., *Braj Vaibhav*. Mathura, Bharati Anusandhan Bhawan, 1972: 249-251. (Hindi)

1303. **Williams, Joanna G.**
Dentils and the question of wooden origins for the Gupta temple. In Joanna G. Williams, ed., *Kaladarsana*. New Delhi, American Institute of Indian Studies, 1981: 159-163.

BUDDHIST

1304. **Bajpai, K.D.**
Mathura ka 'Devanirmit Bodha' stupa. In Kamta Prasad Jain, ed., *Shri Mahavira commemoration volume*, Vol. 1. Agra, Mahavira Jain Society, 1948-49: 188-191. (Hindi)

1305. **Grover, Satish**
The architecture of India: Buddhist and Hindu. New Delhi, Vikas Publishing House, 1980.

1306. **Mitra, Debala**
Buddhist monuments. Calcutta, Sahitya Samsad. 1971.

1307. **Mitterwallner, Gritli Von**
Two stupa basements of Mathura of the 4th and 5th centuries A.D. In Anna Libera Dallapiccola and Stephanie Zingel-ave Lallemant, ed., *The Stupa: Its religious, historical and architectural significance*. Wiesbaden, Franz Steiner Verlag, 1980: 72-89.

JAINA

1308. **Buhler, G.**
A legend of the Jaina stupa at Mathura. *Indian Antiquary*, Vol. 27, 1898: 49-54.

1309. **Fuhrer, A.**
Indo-Scythic architecture and sculpture of the Mathura School. *Journal of Indian Art*, Vol. 5, 1894: 58.

1310. **Jain, Balchandra**
Mathura ka devanirmita stupa. *Prachya Pratibha*, Vol. 3, No. 1, January 1975: 78-81. (Hindi)

1311. **Jain, Jyoti Prasad**
The Jaina architecture—ancient and mediaeval. In *Chotte Lal Jain Smriti granth.* Calcutta, Babu Chotte Lal Jain Abhinandan Samiti, 1967: 35-42.

1312. **Jain, Kamta Prasad**
514 Digambara Jaina stupas at Mathura. *Indian Historical Quarterly*, vol. 6, No. 2, June 1930: 376-377.

1313. **Joshi, N.P.**
Jaina stupa aur puratattva. In Kamta Prasad Jain, ed., *Shri Mahavira commemoration volume*, Vol. 1. Agra, Mahavira Jain Society, 1948-49: 183-187. (Hindi)

1314. **Krishna Deva and Joshi, M.C.**
North India. In A. Ghosh, ed., *Jaina art and architecture*, Vol. 1. New Delhi, Bharatiya Jnanpith, 1974: 143-151.

1315. **Mehta, Mohan Lal**
Jaina kala evam sathapattya. *Shraman*, Vol. 30, No. 3, January 1979: 3-9. (Hindi)

1316. **Nahata, Agar Chand**
Mathura ke Jain stupadiki yatra ke mahatvapurna ullekh. *Anekant*, vol. 12, No. 9, February 1954: 288-293. (Hindi)

1317. **Tandon, O.P.**
Jaina shrines in India. New Delhi, Publications Divisions, 1986.

PAINTING

1318. **Chaturvedi, Balmukund**
Braj ki chitrakala. In Radhey Shyam Dwivedi, ed., *Braj Vaibhav*. Mathura, Bharati Anusandhan Bhawan, 1972: 168-172. (Hindi)

1319. **Khandalavala, Karl, Moti Chandra** and **Pramod Chandra**
Miniature painting: A catalogue of the exhibition of the Sri Motichand Khajanchi collection held by the Lalit Kala Akademi, 1960. New Delhi, Lalit Kala Akademi, 1960.

1320. **Mishra, H.K.**
Preservation of mural paintings at Kusum van Sarovar Mathura. *Bulletin of Museums and Archaeology in U.P.*, Nos. 35-36, June-December 1985: 65-69.

1321. **Mittal, Prabhu Dayal**
Mathura ki lok chitrakala. *Bulletin of Museums and Archaeology in U.P.*, Nos. 15-16, June-December 1975: 1-14. (Hindi)

1322 A palm-leaf painting of Gauranga Mahaprabhu, district Mathura. *Indian Archaeology: A Review*, 1980-81: 95.

MUSIC AND DANCE

1323. **Dwivedi, Radhey Shyam**
Braj ka pracheen sangit aur sangitagya. In Radhey Shyam Dwivedi, ed., *Braj Vaibhav*. Mathura, Bharati Anusandhan Bhawan, 1972: 203-206. (Hindi)

1324. ____.
Braj me khyal goi. In Radhey Shyam Dwivedi, ed., *Braj Vaibhav*. Mathura, Bharati Anusandhan Bhawan, 1972: 216. (Hindi)

1325. **Kailash Chandra**
Braj ki lok-nritya parampara. In Radhey Shyam Dwivedi, ed., *Braj Vaibhav*. Mathura, Bharati Anusandhan Bhawan, 1972: 211-215. (Hindi)

1326. **Misra, Braj Vallabh**
Braj aur nritya-kala. In Radhey Shyam Dwivedi, ed., *Braj Vaibhav*. Mathura, Bharati Anusandhan Bhawan, 1972: 207-210. (Hindi)

1327. **Mittal, Prabhu Dayal**
Braj ki raaslila. Vrindavan, Vrindavan Sodh Sansthan, 1983. (Hindi)

1328. **Shukla, Narendrarai Naval Shankar**
Braj ka Haveli sangeet. In Radhey Shyam Dwivedi, ed., *Braj Vaibhav*. Mathura, Bharati Anusandhan Bhawan, 1972: 179-182. (Hindi)

1329. **Telang, Anand Bihari**
Braj ki sangit parampara. In Radhey Shyam Dwivedi, ed., *Braj Vaibhav*. Mathura, Bharati Anusandhan Bhawan, 1972: 199-202. (Hindi)

MUSEUM

1330. Archaeological Museum, Mathura. *Indian Museums Review*, 1961-64: 54-55

1331. Archaeological Museum, Mathura. *Journal of Indian Museums*, Vol. 11, 1955: 77.

1332. Archaeological Museum, Mathura. *Journal of Indian Museums*, Vol. 12, 1956: 81-83.

1333. **Bajpai, K.D.**
Archaeological Museum, Mathura. *Journal of Indian Museums*, Vol. 5, 1949: 129-130.

1334. _____.
Archaeological Museum, Mathura. *Journal of Indian Museums*, Vol. 6, 1950: 90-92.

1335. _____
Archaeological Museum, Mathura. *Journal of Indian Museums*, Vol. 10, 1954: 44.

1336. **Chanda, Ramaprasad**
Curzon Museum of Archaeology at Mathura. *Archaeological Survey of India Annual Report*, 1930/31-1933/34: 286-289.

1337. **Chaturvedi, J.P.**
Archaeological Museum, Mathura. *Journal of Indian Museums*, Vol. 7, 1951: 72-73.

1338. _____.
Archaeological Museum, Mathura. *Journal of Indian Museums*, Vol. 9, 1953: 184-185.

1339. Curzon Museum of Archaeology, Mathura. *Journal of Indian Museums*, Vol. 4, 1948: 65-67.

1340. The Government Museum, Mathura. *Bulletin of Museums and Archaeology in U.P.*, Nos. 11-12, June-December 1973: I-IV.

1341. Mathura Museum. *Marg*, Vol. 19, No. 1: 25-26.

1342. **Sharma, R.C.**
Archaeological Museum, Mathura. *Journal of Indian Museums*, Vols. 27-28, 1971-1972: 89-92.

1343. _____.
Braj ka vaibhavshali puratattva sangrahalaya. In Radhey Shyam Dwivedi, ed., *Braj Vaibhav*. Mathura, Bharati Anusandhan Bhawan, 1972: 255-262. (Hindi)

1344. _____.
Government Museum, Mathura. *Journal of Indian Museums*, Vols. 32-33, 1976-1977: 123-127.

1345. _____.
Hundred years of the Mathura Museum. *Journal of Indian Museums*, Vol. 29, 1973: 1-8.

1346. _____.
The role of Mathura Museum in community services. In V.P. Dwivedi, ed., *Museums and Museology: New horizons; essays in honour of Dr. Grace Morley on her 80th birthday.* Delhi, Agam Kala Prakashan, 1980: 163-166.

1347. **Srivastava, A.K.**
Government Museums Mathura. *Journal of Indian Museums*, Vol. 36, 1980: 130-132.

1348. **Srivastava, V.N.**
Acquisitions in Mathura Museum. *Bulletin of Museums and Archaeology in U.P.*, No. 2, December 1968: 54-58.

1349. **Trivedi, Shiv Dayal**
Rajkiya Sangrahalaya Mathura. *Uttar Pradesh*, Vol. 2, No. 8, January 1974: 51-53. (Hindi)

AUTHOR INDEX

KEY-WORD INDEX